Anniesland Library

···· Road

Kindfulness

CAROLINE MILLINGTON is an award-winning journalist and media professional. She worked for national magazines such as *Woman's Own* and *Now* for sixteen years before launching a career in television. Caroline currently works as a digital producer at ITV.

This book belongs to…

Who is kind because…

Caroline Millington

Kind ful ness

HEAD of ZEUS

An Anima Book

This is an Anima book, first published in the UK in 2018
by Head of Zeus Ltd

9 7 5 3 1 2 4 6 8

A catalogue record for this book is available from
the British Library.

ISBN (HB): 9781788545389
ISBN (E): 9781788545396

Printed and bound in Great Britain by
CPI Group (UK) Ltd, Croydon CR0 4YY

Head of Zeus Ltd
First Floor East
5–8 Hardwick Street
London EC1R 4RG

WWW.HEADOFZEUS.COM

For my sister, Leanne

Contents

Prologue

This book does not claim to help those experiencing mental health issues such as depression and anxiety. It is not intended to diagnose, treat, cure or prevent any medical condition.

If you want to talk to someone about your mental health – or a loved one's – turn to page 191 where there are details of organizations that can help you. You are not alone.

turn to page 191

* * *

The kindfulness survey took place in 2018.

Kindfulness

On paper, life was good. I had a fantastic job at a national magazine where I'd recently been promoted, had journalism awards on my bookshelf, a wonderful family and smorgasbord of friends to keep me entertained at weekends and evenings. But there were glaring gaps when it came to ticking those 'winning at life' boxes. At least to me.

I spent too much time comparing myself to others who seemed to be climbing the career ladder quicker than Ed Sheeran climbs the charts and smashing their life goals.

There was no boyfriend, let alone a husband.

No pets, let alone kids. I could hear my biological clock quietly ticking away like a time bomb in my womb.

My body image wasn't great.

Something had to change. And it had to be me. More specifically, the way I looked at my life. Because, when it's all a bit 'First World problems' – not the big, serious stuff like grief, unemployment or health issues – the guilt sets in too. So, not only do you feel dissatisfied with life and not good enough, you feel guilty about feeling that way. Which is, quite frankly, pretty shit. Depression and anxiety had hovered around in my life at times in the past, and they were uninvited guests to my future.

I shared my feelings of frustration with a close group of friends, and one recommended her therapist. My decision to go to therapy was simple: you don't wait until you're in the middle of a battle to put your armour on. You don't have to be experiencing mental health issues before you decide to start to look after your mental wellbeing. So I made it a priority.

Little did I realize, this was my first true act of kindfulness.

What is kindfulness?

Let's start with my definition of kindfulness.
I've clearly merged two of my favourite words:

mindfulness *(noun)*
The quality or state of being conscious or aware of
something; a mental state achieved by focusing
one's awareness on the present moment, while
calmly acknowledging and accepting one's
feelings, thoughts and bodily sensations,
used as a therapeutic technique.

kindness *(noun)*
The quality of being friendly, generous and
considerate; a kind act.

My definition of **kindfulness**:
Being conscious, aware and accepting of
one's feelings while demonstrating kindness
and consideration towards oneself. The quality
of being mindfully kind towards oneself and
generous with self-compassion.

Buddhist monk and author Ajahn Brahm described kindfulness as a practice 'that strengthens our ability to look after ourselves – looking after our own minds… to become a kindful force for good in the world.'

Learning to love myself

Talking about yourself feels very self-indulgent. It seems so un-British to pick apart your life when, the reality is, you've got a great one.

I didn't think I was depressed or experiencing anxiety at the time, but I knew that I was in danger of slipping back in that direction. And I could – and should – be happier. What the hell did I have to be fed up about?

I was keen to get to the root of why I felt so frustrated as I unpicked different aspects of my life. It wasn't an overnight epiphany. But therapy allowed me to unravel the tapestry of my life to see the frayed bits, worn patches and holes made from wear and tear – like your favourite pair of jeans that have been destroyed by thigh rub. All those threadbare bits had been worn down because I wasn't making myself a priority; I hadn't been setting personal boundaries; I didn't give myself enough space to grow into the person I wanted to be; and I allowed others to project their issues onto me, absorbing them like an overused bath sponge. I just wasn't kind enough to myself.

In fact, some of the character traits I was so proud of were actually detrimental to my mental and emotional well-being.

Introducing: The People Pleaser

It became clear very quickly that I liked to please. And hated to disappoint people. So guilt was wrapped around acts of kindness, and my priorities were skewed. At work, with family and friends – in every aspect of my life.

Armed with this revelation, I've spent the past couple of years learning to be kinder to myself. I'm so much happier for it. And it's had a positive impact on all my relationships, too.

Kindfulness is not about treading on others to make sure your needs are met first. It's about understanding that it's OK – in fact, absolutely essential – to recognize your own needs and to be vocal about them. It's not about being self-centred but recognizing and acknowledging the negative thoughts you have about yourself and reframing them to be more positive. To love yourself, despite not being society's idea of 'perfect'. And to celebrate who you are instead of comparing yourself to others.

I'd always thought that putting yourself first was selfish. And that friends who were used to getting their own way were self-centred and spoilt. I was wrong. They had learnt to put themselves at the centre of their world – exactly where they should be. Making yourself the most important person in your life, shaking off the idea we're brought up with that we should always put others first, is not about feeding your ego – it's about finding what makes you happy.

What felt self-indulgent at first became a glorious feeling of self-empowerment. Caring for myself felt good. Learning to spot negative patterns in my behaviour or seeing how changing my own priorities and ways of communicating had a positive effect on my relationships with others was uplifting.

You can be kind to yourself and still kick ass.

Kindfulness became like a special savings account – every week I invested time in it, deposited a hefty amount of self-compassion and watched my self-esteem and confidence grow. The more love I invested in myself, the more I had to tap into when I needed it. I could draw on the reserves of positivity and self-worth I'd built up when I made the difficult decision to change jobs; I set firm boundaries in my friendships; and learnt to love my imperfect body. I started to understand what triggers my anxiety, recognize it and work through it.

Investing in yourself costs nothing but time and effort. If you're a caffeine lover like me, think about it as a coffee machine: you make sure you keep it topped up with coffee beans (energy levels), water (body care) and milk (self-compassion) to get the best out of it. Forget to top it up with any of the essentials and it's soon running on empty. And who wants a cup of hot air?

Your happiness should be your number one priority in life. Because it's contagious, and if you make yourself happier you'll be motivated to ensure your loved ones are happy too. Win win.

It's like kindness osmosis. As you become mindfully kinder to yourself – and happier as a result – kindness naturally permeates into all areas of your life, sometimes without the people surrounding you even realizing where the shift has come from.

Being positively selfish

Everyone benefits from kindfulness. That's why putting yourself first is in no way selfish. Treating yourself kindly isn't about stepping over others to get what you want or an excuse to dismiss other people's feelings in pursuit of your own happiness.

Before we can even talk, we're taught to share toys with other children. Keeping what you want is naughty. We're brought up to put other people's feelings first. Even when it hurts us. Many of us grow into adults who are too afraid to speak our minds or ask for what we want in case we offend or are somehow seen as egotistical. And years of swallowing our words can only cause us pain. Kindness is of course key. But not at the expense of our own emotions and feelings.

There may be times when that means going up against a good friend for a job or promotion. Or ending a relationship because you realize it's not enough for you. Or cutting a friend out of your life because they're toxic. Do it all with kindness at the centre of your intentions and you can be confident that you've done the right thing.

This is not a book of magic. In fact, you might even read some sections thinking, 'Er, I know I should be doing that, heard it before.' Great! But just because we know something, doesn't mean we apply it. I'm still very much a work in progress and have to remind myself daily to practise what I preach!

And it's certainly not an excuse to be absent-mindedly selfish, self-centred or arrogant – none of which are kind to yourself or others. It's simply tapping into your own needs and ensuring they are met – either by yourself or by communicating better with others.

This book is no 'one size fits all', so take

away from it what works for you. Ponder on it; dismiss the bits that aren't relevant to your life right now. But I hope you'll cast some serious side-eye at your inner critic in future and stop to think, 'Is that self-criticism really necessary? Am I being kind to myself? Or should I try to change the way I'm thinking about myself in this situation?'

Adulting is exhausting. We juggle a whole host of responsibilities every day, and most of the time don't stop to give ourselves a pat on the back for just getting through a tough day.

So stop giving yourself a hard time.

I hope, by the end of this book, you'll feel empowered to be positively selfish and make the conscious decision to put your own happiness front and centre in your life. Because you are responsible for your own happiness, and you deserve to be happy, and to be loved. You are already enough.

The 10 kindfulness commandments

1. You will stop feeling guilty.

2. You will treat your body with kindness.

3. You will make time for you.

4. You will take regular breaks from your phone and social media.

5. You will be more compassionate towards yourself.

6. You will accept you can't change everything and everybody but you can change yourself.

7. You will put your own needs first and be positively selfish.

8. You will set boundaries in all relationships and friendships.

9. You will love yourself.

10. You will be badass.

You, you, you

The small things are important but self-care is so much more than a bubble bath or having a glass of wine.

Just the word 'self-care' might even make you shudder. To some it sounds 'worthy' and fluffy. But the idea isn't going anywhere and I think we should all embrace whatever version suits you.

Self-care is whatever makes you happy and content. For some it will be having a cup of coffee and reading a good book. For others, it will be making sure they eat healthily and exercise, or cancelling all plans and staying home. And other people will enjoy a cocktail (or seven) and dance the night away!

We all have different needs. So how you apply kindfulness to your life is entirely up to you.

'You have got to love yourself. If you don't, nobody else is going to love you. The way to do that is with acts of self-love. Look after your body, drink water, take care of yourself. All this helped me when I was in recovery because I hated myself.

My first sponsor told me to get a mirror, keep it by the bed, look in it every day and say 'I love you'. The first time I picked it up I started crying. But over time you get used to saying it. When you love yourself you believe you are worth being looked after. It's taken me a long time to learn that.'

Davina McCall

Taking care of yourself

Make a note of what self-care means to you. What would you like to do more of to take care of your well-being – mentally and physically? Grab your diary and schedule in some self-care time!

You are enough

Self-esteem is the value people place on themselves. During our lifetime it can swing dramatically depending on our personal circumstances.

What we're looking for is an equilibrium. A focus and acceptance that we're enough and we are worthy. So when life smacks us in the face with a challenge, we can process it and work through it.

Self-efficacy is the ability to achieve personal goals – not someone else's we're comparing ourselves to on social media, and not those set by society at large who can dictate which body part is in fashion this year and might not be your greatest asset (you look amazing today, by the way, just in case no one has told you yet!) or the same goals of your friendship group.

Success looks different to everyone. And your list of dreams and goals will be completely different to other people's – even your best friends.

Academic researchers have found a strong link between self-efficacy and success – if you believe you can reach your goal, you're more likely to reach it.

Believe in yourself

'I can't'... well, this is awkward, because you CAN. Want something hard enough and you'll make it happen.

Be prepared for forks in the road, lessons along the way, and maybe even a reimagining of that dream. You're free to adapt your goal, scrap it and start another one.

Split your ultimate goal into mini-goals. A wise friend once told me, 'How do you eat an elephant? One bite at a time.'

Surround yourself with positivity. It's time to sack off the naysayers. If friends or family question your ability, just tell them 'Watch me!' Do not let people's doubts penetrate your bubble of positivity.

Banish the negativity. Take inspiration from Chumbawamba's *Tubthumping* – a big anthem back in the glory year of 1997. Knocked down?

Get back up again. And listen to *This Is Me* from *The Greatest Showman* soundtrack for a positivity anthem.

Don't be self-pitying. We all know someone who puts themselves down all the time. They are constantly throwing themselves a pity party and you're invited. Bring a bottle! 'Come on in while I tell you what a terrible life I'm having. I'm not pretty enough. Everyone is horrible to me. I'm lonely. It's everyone else's fault, not mine.' Never mind their glass being half full – they've downed it, drained the last drop and left it upside down on the drainer by the sink to make sure it's bone dry. Don't be that person. Make a vow to yourself right now to stop making self-pitying remarks. You don't deserve them.

Self-compassion

We often lack self-compassion. If a friend comes to you with a problem or worry, we're happy to sit and talk to them about it, look at ways we can solve any issue and tell them how great they are and how brilliant their future will be.

When it comes to my friends, I'm the first person to slip into a cheerleading outfit, grab my pom-poms and start cheering them on as they make difficult life decisions or overcome an emotional obstacle.

We should look and speak to ourselves through the eyes of those who love us most. When I'm having a bad day, I try to channel how my best friend would speak to me and give myself a positive pep talk.

It's time to stop berating yourself and treat yourself like you would treat your best friend instead.

Don't put things off until tomorrow

'Zengo saidan' is a Zen Japanese expression which means, 'Do not worry about yesterday because you cannot change it, and do not worry about tomorrow because it has not come yet.'

Basically, there's no point regretting what happened yesterday – it's gone. And there's no point worrying about tomorrow, it's unpredictable and you can't plan for everything. We spend too much time thinking about the past or future and forget to live in the present. What can you do TODAY to be kind to yourself?

We all need a kick up the arse on occasion. Sometimes I feel like even *Scandal*'s Olivia Pope and her team of gladiators would have trouble tracking down my motivation.

Try to get in the habit of getting things done today. You're only fooling yourself if you put things off. Tempted to procrastinate? Give yourself a 10-second rule. Count to 10 and get going. I work well to deadlines so if you do too, set yourself a deadline and stick to it! And reward yourself for good behaviour. A toddler-style sticker chart might not appeal, but give yourself 30 minutes to relax, watch an episode of your favourite TV show, or have a nap. I regularly bribe myself to get stuff done!

'We are what we repeatedly do.
Excellence, then, is not an act,
but a habit.'

Will Durant

Kindfulness survey

You say...

What acts of kindness do you show yourself?

- 'Meditating and going to the gym.'
- 'I write down my thoughts every day. I try to laugh and smile as much as I can.'
- 'Resting, keeping my home lovely, nice food, holidays, down time, self-praise.'
- 'The occasional day in bed, giving myself a break from my life.'
- 'Having a bath, allowing myself to watch trashy TV without feeling guilty, cutting myself some slack.'
- 'Putting on make-up, which is rare with young kids.'
- 'Films, books, baths, chocolate.'
- 'Going to church.'
- 'Regular exercise, eating well and sleeping well.'
- 'Weekly Pilates class and seeing friends to laugh with.'
- 'Having down time, mani/pedi, brunch with friends.'

Putting yourself first

You know when you're on a plane and they're running you through the safety instructions in case of emergency? There's a reason you're told to put your oxygen mask on before helping others.

We instinctively want to help others first – especially children – but you're no use to anyone if you don't look after yourself as a priority.

This is the perfect example of being positively selfish. At first, it can feel unnatural or uncomfortable – but you are entitled to put your own needs first and foremost. Because, once you feel like you've got a grip on life, when you're happy with the decisions you're making and the direction you're taking, your happiness will be projected into all other areas of your life. I've seen it for myself – in my relationships, my career and my self-esteem.

One of my very good friends isn't afraid to speak up. She always gets what she wants because she's forthright in telling you. I love her to death but found it incredibly frustrating that we would always do what she wanted without much consideration for what I wanted. Until I realized she wasn't the problem – I was. She wasn't demanding because she wanted anyone else to feel bad – in fact, the thought would mortify her. She just isn't afraid to say what she wants, and she expects to get it. I, on the other hand, would sit back and go with the flow, only to end up missing out because I wouldn't speak up. Asking for what you want doesn't have to be confrontational, so there's no need to shy away from piping up.

Since finding my voice, making myself heard and communicating what I want, our friendship is better than ever. It's on a more equal footing.

Too many of us are suffering in silence. Out of politeness or guilt. And we're the only ones who can say something.

Don't want to go to that party? 'Thanks so much for the invite but I've got a really busy week and won't be able to make it this time.'

Carving out your own path at work? 'This is the direction I'd like to develop in so I'd like to turn down the opportunity of that project. Can we look at my goals for the year and agree on a development path?'

Single and fed up? 'The best is yet to come…'

I'm not bossy,
I'm the boss!

So, you're reading this book because you know you deserve MORE. More self-worth, more self-compassion, more happiness. More of the good stuff. And I hope my experiences, insights and advice help you make the changes you need. Because YOU have the power. You're the CEO of your own life.

It's so easy to become frustrated in life because the people around us don't seem to be in on our master plan to happiness. The boss who won't give you the promotion you deserve. The person you fancy who has erected an emotional 'friend zone' to keep you hanging about on the platonic plateau. Or your partner who you feel takes you for granted.

But don't play the blame game. Don't be a victim. Because you can't control other people's actions and opinions. Stepping into your own power – like slipping on your favourite heels or lacing up your trainers – and taking responsibility for your own happiness gives you a sense of pride that no one else's opinion can.

A few rules I've introduced into my kindful-ness life:

- **Even when I like a guy, I try my best not to do the chasing.** I spent too many years pining after 'just good friends' who paid me just a little bit too much attention to keep me hanging on. I am no longer anyone's back-up or platonic puff piece to be kept around as an ego boost.

- **I won't feel guilty about saying no to anyone.** It's just a word. And I believe an upfront 'No, sorry, I can't/It's not for me/I'd rather not' is better than a late cancellation or disappointment.

- **Create your own career plan.** Don't wait to be given permission or told what your next step should be. I switched from editing magazines to being a digital and social media producer in television, and then wrote this book. And I doubt I'll stop there! Do not let anyone label you or box you in. And if someone tells you it's too difficult to change from your career lane to another: mirror, signal, manoeuvre onto a different motorway!

- **You get to make every decision.** The responsibility can be daunting but it's also empowering. Revel in it. Because when you apply kindfulness to life, you get to take all the successes and credit.

- **Take charge.** Make those executive decisions. Kick it off with a life performance development review…

Your kindfulness personal development review

At work we're used to having annual or bi-annual performance development reviews to check in with our boss, get feedback on how we're doing and discuss future goals. And we should be doing the same with our own lives.

Grab a piece of paper and a pen and do your own PDR right now.

Review your personal life and career in the past year – identifying successes, problems you had to overcome and things you learnt. Take all the time you need to consider the most important areas of your life. And feel free to add your own to the below.

And remember – do this with kindfulness! Be honest but not overly critical. Think of the successes and achievements. This is an opportunity to design a brighter, happier future for yourself, not rip your self-esteem to shreds.

General life

What do you want to keep doing, what do you want to stop doing and what do you want to start doing?

Are there any changes – big or small – you want to make to your life?

Are there any big conversations you want to have but have been putting off?

What opportunities can you create for yourself to increase your happiness?

Who are the people in your life that can support you to get there?

And finally, what are you doing brilliantly at that you're proud of?

Emotional well-being

How have you been feeling? Are there any mental health issues you'd like to address? What makes you happy?

Body

What is your relationship like with food, drink and exercise? Is there anything you're doing too much or too little of and would like to change? Do you love your body? Write a list of all the awesome things your body does and show it the compassion it deserves.

Relationship/marital status

If you're in a relationship: Are you happy? Do you feel valued? Are there any changes you would make to improve it? Are you ensuring your own needs are being met? Do you need to work on communicating?

If you're single: Are you happy? Do you feel worthy of love? Are you putting yourself out there to find it? What's stopping you? Do you know what you're looking for in a partner?

Friendships

Are you putting enough effort into your friendships? Is there anyone toxic you need to cull from your life? Would you like to make more friends and how can you do that?

Parenting

How can you be kinder to yourself as a parent? Do you have enough quality time with your child? What have been your proudest parenting moments in the past year? Are you making enough time for yourself as a person and not just as a parent?

Work

Are you happy at work? What have you achieved in the past year that you're proud of? What are your ambitions for the next year? What areas do you need to improve on and how can you get there? Are you dealing with any difficult work relationships and how can you change them?

Time for you

Are you happy with the amount of time you have to yourself on a weekly basis? Do you have 'me time' scheduled in your diary?

Start now!

We'll be looking at all these areas of your life in the following chapters in more detail, and will come back to your PDR at the end of the book so you can add to it again. Keep your PDR in a safe place and check it in six months – then do a new one.

Remember, you don't need to be a hot mess to make improvements. You might feel you're pretty happy with your lot. But I believe there's always an extra 10% of happiness available for anyone looking for it. And the only person who can make it happen is you.

Inventor of the light bulb, Thomas Edison, was asked about the many thousands of failures he had when trying to create the light bulb and said, 'I have not failed. I've just found 10,000 ways that don't work'.

If you can accept that mistakes and failures are just part of your journey to success, you'll have a much more positive outlook. I've applied for jobs I haven't got and accepted that it just wasn't meant to be. Instead of beating myself up and looking at what I didn't have to get that position, I looked at what I *did* have, and created a new list of challenges and goals to work towards. I've had relationships fail (haven't we all!) but rather than blame myself, I took a lesson from every dating disaster and decided they gave me a more defined idea of the kind of man I deserve and relationship I want. Sometimes, it's not you, it really is them!

Treat yourself kindfully and you'll get to where you're supposed to be with a unique set of life lessons.

3

Making changes

Change. It's a small word that makes the best of us shudder.

A fear of change is called 'metathesiophobia' (good for pub quiz knowledge – you're welcome!). It comes from the Greek 'meta' meaning 'change' and 'phobos' meaning fear. And while some people suffer from extreme versions of this, many of us will admit that we're not fans of doing things differently, at work or at home. Our brains are just not wired to embrace change. It's why habits form so easily and are hard to break.

But change is actually good for you! It just depends on your attitude and how you break things down. Because you can 'trick' your brain to change if you really want to. I'm talking about changing habits not addictive behaviour, which is obviously a far more serious lifestyle change to tackle.

Have you ever been on a diet? Or tried to give up booze for a bit? Or taken up exercise?

Diets tend to fail because they are a huge lifestyle overhaul which people don't enjoy and are unsustainable.

Going on a diet = hard.

Introducing healthier food into your meals = easier.

We're creatures of habit. Most of us tend to rotate our favourite meals week in and week out. Despite a wardrobe full of clothes, we'll pick the same outfits for work again and again. We go to the same restaurants, walk the same route to work and watch the same TV shows. It's in our nature to repeat behaviour that makes us feel good.

And our brains are overwhelmed with decision-making in this modern age. Just wander through the supermarket and you can see the variety of food, drink and entertainment on offer.

And in this multi-media age, we're showered with outside stimuli constantly.

But we CAN change. Neuroplasticity is the ability of the brain to change its physical structure and function based on input from your experiences, behaviours, emotions, and even thoughts. Neuroplasticity is the 'muscle building' part of the brain. When we do something all the time, we become stronger at it. Having a thought or doing an action over and over again increases its power – like driving or riding a bicycle, it becomes automatic. If something is repeated often enough, it reinforces a neural pathway and changes how our brain works. We literally become what we think and do.

Ralph Waldo Emerson, who led the transcendentalist movement of the mid-nineteenth century, said, 'You are what you think all day long.' You literally are what you think. So, repetitive behaviour and thought patterns become who we are. If they're negative, we become negative.

But you have the capacity to change that and retrain your brain with effort and perseverance. And, I promise, there is nothing better than making positive changes to your life.

Procrastinator or perfectionist?

Ah, good old procrastination. I could have a PhD in it. It's one of my worst habits. But, applying kindfulness, I realize that I don't put off doing things because I'm lazy. It's because of a fear of failure. I have applied delaying tactics to so many areas of my life over the years – dating, weight loss, going for promotions or changing jobs – not because I wasn't motivated or didn't have the desire, but because I was scared of failing. In the past, I've stayed in jobs for far too long because the thought of having to put myself out there and risk rejection was too much to think about. And often it's when you're feeling at your lowest that you are least likely to make that change, because you just can't face feeling any worse than you do. But putting off those difficult conversations – asking for a pay rise, ending a relationship – just prolongs your misery in the long run.

It's natural to have an emotional reaction to change. Sometimes we might not even be conscious of having a negative reaction. But, chances are, if you're putting off doing something and it's not due to lack of time, you're procrastinating because the task has provoked an emotional reaction.

The good news? According to *Psychology Today*, perfectionists are often procrastinators: 'It is psychologically more acceptable to never tackle a task than to face the possibility of falling short on performance.'

Now I tend to think, 'What's the worst that can happen?' Imagine the best version of you, the confident person you dream of being (and will be!) and what they would do in the situation you're facing. Write it down! If you really want something, the only person stopping you from going to get it is yourself. Visualize taking on the challenge and doing it brilliantly. Close your eyes and picture yourself succeeding and feeling great about it. You've got the power to make that happen.

If you want a promotion, list the reasons you deserve it and take the list in when you speak to your manager. The worst that can happen: they say no and you ask to have another conversation in six months. You have nothing to lose.

Desperate to expand your network but worried you'll look desperate or foolish? You won't! Jot down all the reasons why people should want to work with you, all your achievements in the past year and goals you're working towards. Keep the list on your phone and read it over before any networking event or big work meeting. Remind yourself of just how awesome you are. If you don't ask, you don't get.

And if it's dating you're stuck on, ask your best friends to send you all the reasons you're totally datable. Read it over and over again before going on a date and believe every word. Dating is a numbers game and you have to keep kissing those frogs before you meet your prince/princess.

So, if like me you're one of life's procrastinators, take pride in the fact that you're a perfectionist who just wants to do a good job and stop putting off things that could be amazing!

Mis-behaving

You form habits by doing the same thing over and over again – both good and bad behaviour. When you have the desire to do something and succeed, dopamine is released to reward you and make you feel good. It motivates you to repeat the behaviour in the future because you know it makes you feel great.

But, with effort, you can change your habits. It just takes time – longer than the 21 days usually quoted as the period necessary to form a new habit. There's a 'three-plus-nine-week willpower rule' because it takes three weeks to establish new behaviour – then you have to repeat that behaviour for nine weeks to turn it into a habit.

And if you're going to fail, fail well. Take those lessons with you, brush yourself down and try another way. I believe most things in life happen for a reason. If you failed, it wasn't meant for you but probably taught you something along the way. Try a different path. Believe in yourself.

There is always room for improvement. Whether it's your self-esteem, career, relationships or body, there's no end to the possibilities when you have an open mind and heart.

Strive – not for perfection – but for the best you can be and can get out of life. This is about YOU. Not someone else's idea of a good life. Because we're all different, and my idea of a perfect day will be completely different to yours.

Mine involves copious cups of tea, walking under a clear blue sky, laughing with friends, tucking into some tasty food, listening to some Eighties classics and binge-watching *Scandal* before getting a good night's sleep. It's the simple things!

Forming new habits is a bit like learning to drive a car. At first it's incredibly daunting remembering pedals, gears, mirrors and indicators. But, just like learning to drive, the more you practise a new habit, the easier it becomes and soon it's like second nature.

As children, we learn new habits every day. Walking, potty training, falling asleep by ourselves, reading and writing. It's second nature to learn and develop, trying new things and challenging ourselves.

So why are we so hesitant when it comes to creating new habits in our personal lives? We're creatures who like routine.

Stop waiting for the perfect time to introduce change and start today.

'We do not need magic to change
the world, we carry all the power
we need inside ourselves already:
we have the power to imagine better.'

J. K. Rowling

What changes do you want to make?

Take 10 minutes to think about the changes – big and small – you'd like to make to your life: your love life, career, body, friends, free time.

Write down some goals you'd like to achieve this year. Think about what it will take to get there and who can help you. Then put a plan together. Change doesn't have to be hard but it's good to have support and a clear focus.

Visualization is used by many people to make changes and focus on what they want to achieve. Some create vision boards with words and pictures of their future goals. I keep a book with lists of ambitions, positive mantras, words, pictures and doodles. I stick in tickets to events I've loved so it's packed with positivity and dreams.

What's the easiest change you could make? Start that one today. Once you've formed a new habit and are comfortable in it, then start the next one. Be kind to yourself if you slip back – it takes time.

How to change

Changing your behaviour and habits isn't easy, but it can be done. Here's how your brain can help…

◆ **Reduce stress**
Often we cling onto bad habits to deal with stress – smoking, drinking, fast food, too much TV and not enough fresh air. We create our own coping skills but they're not always beneficial apart from keeping worry at bay, and even then they don't always work. Exercise, sleep, yoga and meditation can all help deal with signs of stress.

◆ **Reach out for support**
According to research, behaviour and feelings are contagious. So if you want to make a change, find a friend to do it with you. As soon as I cut back on the booze I found friends wanted to do the same. We started having sober dinners instead of boozy nights out. I stopped going out as much, but the time I do spend with mates is quality time catching up instead of trying to

shout into each other's ears in a noisy club. It's brunch instead of bar hopping. More walks in the park, less lunchtime mimosas.

Whatever change you want to make – take up a new hobby, do 10,000 steps a day, switch to decaf coffee – see if anyone wants to do it with you.

◆ **Trigger-happy**
Something usually happens to lead us to form a habit – conflict, boredom, anxiety. Next time you catch yourself repeating a habit you want to change, take a moment to see what triggered it. Can you avoid or change that?

◆ **Charge up your willpower**
Making changes takes effort. Keep your serotonin – the neurochemical that scientists believe fuels confidence and helps regulate happiness, anxiety and mood – topped up. Sunlight, exercise, vitamin B, St John's Wort and massages can all help raise your serotonin levels.

◆ **One change at a time**
Start small and build up from there. Don't try to overhaul your life in one day and risk feeling

like you're failing at everything. I never 'ban' anything because I know I'll rebel and want to do it/eat it/drink it. Instead, I've managed to make a few changes by recognizing I'm doing something different but that I'm choosing to do it. It's helped me create new habits like cutting back on alcohol, drinking more water and going to bed early. If you feel like you're in control and making a decision because you want to and not because you're being forced to, then in my experience you're more likely to create that good habit and keep it up. Take it a day at a time, too. And if you slip up, just remember you can start again tomorrow.

◆ Live in the moment

Pay attention to what you're doing. Sometimes the best way to break a habit is to create a new, healthier one. The kinder we are to ourselves and our bodies, the more likely we are to make better decisions and step out of negative, repetitive behaviour patterns. Congratulate yourself when you keep following the change. Remind yourself you're doing something good for you and that you deserve the best.

Choosing to change

Performance life coach and Neuro Linguistic Programming practitioner **Mary Meadows** says...

The most important relationship we have in our lives is the one we have with ourselves. This isn't stuff they teach you at school – yet – and most of our parents only taught us how to handle relationships with others. I'm yet to meet a woman whose mother taught her how to love themselves first.

We live in a world where 'busy' is glorified, so no wonder we have the perceived idea that we don't have time for this 'self-love' stuff. So how do you teach yourself?

Start

Become conscious to the idea that something needs to change. Look for a tipping point. Sometimes it's a dramatic one like exhaustion or illness. Other times it might be a conversation or reading a book such as this one.

Take note

Notice a behaviour, a habit, a thought process, a relationship that no longer serves you. Keeping a gentle curiosity is the most helpful here – you didn't know what you didn't know.

Choose

Then you have a choice. You could stay in that comfortable place and go back to being unconscious; waiting for change can become a habit – waiting for spring, waiting for after the holiday, waiting for Monday. Or... you could START NOW.

Focus

What can you bring into your life, rather than 'stopping' anything? Focus on what you can control and ignore what you can't. Most change starts with a conversation – usually a hard one with yourself or with others. Don't be scared: think of the possibilities and your future.

Reflection

Choose to reflect daily, weekly or monthly. It's very simple – anyone can do it and it encourages you to notice your feelings, thought patterns and emotional responses to everyday life and put a plan in place. Grab a pen and notebook, and reflect on the following:

1 What went well?
2 What didn't go as well?
3 What am I going to do more of?
4 What am I going to do less of?

They can be one-word answers or pages and pages – there are no rules! Kindfulness is possible, but it takes a bit of bravery, a bit of courage, a bit of 'badassery'. But START – nothing changes if nothing changes.

It's all in your mind...

What's the difference between thoughts and feelings? And can you influence either or both?

They feed into each other: happy thoughts = happy mood; negative thoughts = bad mood. Our feelings are how we know how to react to a situation. I recently felt anxiety creep up on me and nestle in the pit of my stomach, curled up like an extremely heavy and unwelcome cat. Like Grumpy Cat but huge, mean and uncomfortable.

I recognized it was there but refused to feed it. I knew it had been triggered by stress so could only deal with it the best way I knew how:

distract myself with work, play some classic Eighties songs and create all the happy feelings I could.

I told people I was feeling anxious but carried on with life and took care of myself with good food and cups of tea.

That big, fat cat comes and goes and I don't always have control of him. But I acknowledge him each time, then refuse to give him food for thought. Eventually he slopes off to wherever he came from, leaving me feeling lighter and happy without a strange feline sense of dread.

Researchers say we have between 50,000 and 70,000 thoughts a day. And up to 98% of those thoughts can be exactly the same as the ones we had the day before. It's also believed that 80% of our thoughts are negative. That's the same negative thoughts spinning round our heads day in day out, without us even realizing.

Human beings naturally sway towards the negative. The 'negativity bias' enables us to be alerted to danger or threat more easily. It was key to our survival, but these days the threats we fret about are mostly in our minds.

The trick is to recognize the negativity that's

not serving a good purpose, acknowledge it and send it on its way, encouraging more positive thoughts. I now catch myself when I'm being self-critical. Next time you notice yourself think, 'I'm useless for not doing xyz' or comparing yourself to others, 'I should be doing more…' – stop, pause and reframe. 'I haven't done xyz because I've been busy doing abc. I'm doing the best I can.' And 'I'm doing enough. I can't compare myself to anyone else because I don't know what they're juggling in their lives.' Everything in context. Sometimes just getting through the day without spilling food down my top is enough to make me feel like I'm winning at life, even if I haven't replied to every work email/done the washing-up. I still have negative thoughts, but I try my best not to let them imprint on my brain long enough to stress me out.

Research has shown that learning to identify less with your thoughts and feelings by noting them as they come and go can reduce the intensity of feelings of stress and worry by up to 50%. And the more you practise, the easier it gets.

Picture this: I'm stuck in a defeatist thought loop – a mini-me drives a stream of negative thoughts through my mind while flicking V-signs at whatever inspired idea, positive thought or content emotion I'm feeling.

Yes, my 'inner voice' is mocking me while performing donuts in a flash convertible. But my good old negative thought policewoman steps into the road holding up a STOP sign. Cynical mini-me grinds to a halt, chastised, and slowly drives away looking sheepish – leaving me to develop and embrace the brilliant idea/positive thinking or wonderful emotion.

If you haven't got one already, it's time to employ your very own negative thought police to help patrol your thought patterns and step into your mind map to help filter the negative.

With practise, you'll soon identify those self-doubting drivers honking their horns to distract you from self-praise, and the negative thought police will recognize, acknowledge them and send them off in another direction.

Think of it as a bit like *Wacky Races* for the mind!

Unpicking bad habits takes time, but it is possible. My mind is no longer like Mario Kart, at least.

Your negative thought police

Put your negative thought police to good use and practice. Write a list of all the things you'd like to achieve in the next year – big and small. It could be doing your 10,000 steps a day, getting a promotion at work, tidying your bedroom more often, travelling to a new country, meditating every day. Notice what thoughts you have around each goal and practise reframing those that are negative…

Well, that's never going to happen = I could work towards making that happen.

No one is going to promote me = I deserve a promotion and am going to discuss my career path with my boss.

I'm just too lazy to be bothered = I've got a busy life and am doing the best I can.

I can't = I can.

Do not be your own worst enemy. If someone else stops you from chasing your dream, you can look at taking another path they're not blocking. But if YOU'RE the one person standing in the way of your own happiness, you need to swap the negative for the positive.

Banish the self-doubt

Let's start with the decision to write this book. I had the idea way back in 2016. And did nothing. Zilch. Nada. If something is going to benefit ONLY me, I'll take my time, mull it over, push it to the back of my mind, tell a few people, pretend I never mentioned it, and so on.

So what was holding me back from putting the idea down on paper? Self-doubt. Who would want to read what I've got to say about being kind to yourself?

I'm not qualified to tell people what to do.

It's a bit arrogant to think anyone would want to read this.

Just don't bother.

I mean, how RUDE am I to myself? And I bet you've had similar conversations with yourself about things you'd like to do. I had a serious word with myself, wrote a 3,000-word book proposal and approached a friend of a friend who is a book agent and who loved the idea. The rest, as they say, is history.

Kindfulness is still a work in progress for me.

I have to work hard to be kinder to myself every day.

Reframing your thoughts

Research shows that if you want to feel happy, you have to focus on your own wishes and desires, as well as those of others.

A study of more than 3,000 people found a link between self-compassion and four key areas of health: eating, exercise, stress and sleep.

The concept of being positively selfish is one I've fully embraced – and you should too, without feeling guilty about it!

So it's time to start concentrating on your own moments of joy – letting go of the stress, making sure you get enough sleep, eating well and moving more.

There's so much pressure to feel like you should be chasing up that career ladder like you're appearing on TV's *Ninja Warrior*. And what about your personal life? If your Instagram feed isn't full of perfectly posed photos in exotic locations, an avocado on toast brunch with your beautiful friends and fun, fun, fun nights out with cocktails (but not a hangover in sight the next day, just 'I woke up like this' bedhead) – then you're failing at life. #InstaSmug

No, no, NO.

When did it stop being OK to be happy with your lot? We became ashamed of what we have and are always looking for the next thing – what's next? What's next? More, more, more…

Life can be overwhelming. Whatever your personal situation, everything is in context. You are no better or worse than anyone else, and everyone has different limits when it comes to dealing with stress.

Ah yes. Stress. Even the most identifiable problem can have a knock-on effect and ruin a perfectly good day.

Car broken down?

Child refusing to get ready on time for school?

Boss cancels a meeting at work?

Friend late for dinner?

None of these are the end of the world, but

if you're not looking after your emotional well-being they can certainly feel that way.

The 'C' word

Control. Or rather lack of it – which can send many of us spiralling in our mind. Lack of control is one of my biggest triggers when it comes to feeling anxious and having negative thoughts. Whether it's friends and family, a work situation or travelling, stressful situations often arise when there's a feeling of not being in control – or clashing over who is in control.

The definition of control: the power to influence or direct people's behaviour or the course of events.

The term 'control freak' is thrown around a lot but, for me, it's not about exerting my control over others but having the power to determine the course of events in my own life. And, of course, that's not always possible. There are many instances when you have no control over something happening in your life. There are rules and regulations we abide by every day without even thinking about it. But in our own domain – are we really the king or queen of everything we see?

During therapy I learnt how to take control of a situation because, being a natural people pleaser, saying 'no' or facing a confrontational situation doesn't come easy to me. Accept the things you can't control: the weather, when a baby is born (most of the time), death (sad but true), taxes, not always getting the boy/girl...

But what you CAN control is how you react to these things. Growing frustration with your personal situation can have a huge negative impact on your mental well-being. If you feel every day is a battle, that is going to be exhausting. Applying kindfulness can help keep the feelings of helplessness and hopelessness at bay.

Accepting you can't control other people or every situation, but that you can control the way in which you react and communicate your needs and feelings, is key.

Take 10 minutes

We're so busy in our day-to-day lives that it's easy to forget to check in with ourselves. When people ask how we are, we brush it off with a 'Fine thanks.' When was the last time you thought about how you are? Really thought about it?

It could be first thing in the morning while having a shower – always the best place to contemplate your navel – or last thing at night instead of scrolling through social media for the 4,386th time that day.

How are you feeling?

Have you got any worries niggling and what can you do to solve any problems?

What positive things can you do today?

Do you need to let go of any negative issues you've had and chalk it up to experience?

To do – YOU!

Start the day by making a doable 'to-do' list. This is a list of daily goals that you want to achieve,

NOT 'win the lottery, book 10 appointments, write a presentation and do all the washing'.

By writing a list of things you want to do, and ticking them off, you'll have an instant sense of satisfaction and pride. The big stuff should be on a separate list.

At the end of the day, check your list and tick things off, move them into the next day or scrap them completely. But seriously, creating a 'to-do' list is a must for those embracing kindfulness, even if you only ever have a wish list with no deadline to miss! So, you've probably got the point – I love a list. And I'm not the only one.

Psychologist and author, Dr David Cohen, believes that we love 'to-do' lists because they quell anxiety about the chaos of life; give us a structure and a plan to stick to; and are proof of what we have achieved that day, week or month.

A study from Wake Forest University, North Carolina, showed that just planning tasks that we need to do can free us from feeling anxious: 'Simply writing the tasks down will make you more effective.'

Embracing the 'to-do' list is a key kindfulness strategy. It enables you to take control of what you need to do and lessens any anxiety surrounding how long the list is, as well as giving clarity to what you NEED to do and what is NICE to do (these are the two columns on my list). You also get a sense of accomplishment every time you cross something off the list.

My Grampy used to tease my sister and I by saying, 'Mañana, Mañana' when we were putting off doing something we'd said we'd do. Although he was Welsh, not Spanish, strangely enough.

What are you putting off? What are you scared of? Thinking about the task and why you're hesitant to tackle it can help you work through your worries and tackle it head on.

Lists have another important role to play: they can help you check in with yourself, note your goals and your frustrations.

Sitting down with any of your lists and going through them while being in the moment and seeing what feelings are evoked is a great way to see what areas of your life need some more attention.

If your work 'to-do' list makes you want to weep or enrages you every time you look at it, the kindful thing to do would be to ask for a meeting with your manager and discuss your workload.

As a manager, I often worked with members of the team on how they could make their workload easier, time management, and what, if anything, could be delegated. My work mantra is: work smarter, not harder. A good manager should always be happy to talk through any workload issues. After all, it's far better to flag up that there's too much to do before deadlines are missed.

Lists for life

My lists are as follows:*

Goals and dreams

My life list. The things I'd like to work towards. 'Big' things – some have been ticked off (get a mortgage, go on safari) and some have not (get married, get a cat). The BIG list is something you can return to every year and tweak.

Must do – the little list

Today. As soon as possible. The little list is 'do these things in the next 48 hours and I'm winning at life'. Little wins = big happiness.

Need to do – the big list

Actual, practical things I need to do in the near future. Life administration list ('life-min' if you will). These are not 'today urgent' but necessary things that generally include: smear test, book

---

*   Fancy stationery optional, but life is always better with a kick-ass notebook/pad. Throw in a highlighter and I'd probably marry you.

car in for a service, dentist, research insurance, look for a new job (optional). Try to tick at least one 'big list' thing off a week.

Nice to do – the fun list

Buy best friend's birthday present, research holiday possibilities, and so on

Office to-do – work

Work lists are kept totally separate from life lists, and the two should not cross on paper, iPhone notes or post-it notes. Work tasks should not encroach on your personal time – keeping the lists separate should help you keep a work/life balance.

If your work tasks don't get finished in work hours, unless it's a special project and you've agreed to go above and beyond on this occasion, they should roll into the next day. And if there's a problem with that, see Chapter 10 on using kindfulness in the workplace!

Mindfulness

In the past few years, mindfulness – the quality or state of being conscious or aware of something – has become increasingly popular and is now mainstream, recommended by doctors and psychologists and used in schools and business corporations worldwide. Apple allows a 30-minute break for meditation. Nike has a 'quiet' room for it, too. While mindfulness is living in the moment and being aware of whatever activity you're doing or taking in your surroundings, meditation is the focusing of your mind to achieve a mental clarity and a sense of calmness.

Even if the idea of meditating every day seems

a step too far, the concept of mindfulness – focusing your attention on the present moment and noticing what's happening in the here and now – is easily applied, and one of the most useful tools in exploring your emotional well-being. Apps such as Headspace; Calm; Stop, Breathe & Think; Buddhify; and Welzen all come highly recommended. And everyone can find 10 minutes in their day to use mindfulness if they want to.

If you're upset, stressed or anxious, sitting in the moment and noticing your feelings and exploring them helps identify triggers or behavioural patterns. This, in turn, enables us to make positive changes.

Some people swear by meditation. I've floated out of meditation classes feeling calm and centred, and I try to use a meditation app on a regular basis (I'm working on every day!). Studies have shown that regular meditation can decrease stress and anxiety, boost the immune system and relieve pain. Mindfulness is recommended by the National Institute for Health and Care Excellence (NICE) as a way to prevent depression in people who have had three or more bouts of depression in the past.

Professor Mark Williams, former director of the Oxford Mindfulness Centre, has said that mindfulness means knowing directly what is going on inside and outside ourselves, moment by moment: 'It's easy to lose touch with the way our bodies are feeling and to end up living "in our heads" – caught up in our thoughts without stopping to notice how those thoughts are driving our emotions and behaviour,' he says. 'An important part of mindfulness is an awareness of our thoughts and feelings as they happen moment to moment. It's about allowing ourselves to see the present moment clearly. When we do that, it can positively change the way we see ourselves and our lives.'

For others, weaving mindfulness into everyday tasks like cooking, yoga, painting or walking is the perfect time to mull over how they are feeling emotionally.

Mantras

The power of positive thinking can help you get what you want out of life. Ultimately, that's what kindfulness is all about.

Think about your goals and scribble down mantras that will help keep you on track. Write them on post-its and stick them on your fridge, mirror or front door for daily reminders. Write them on the front of your notebook at work. Set them as your screen saver on your phone. Use positive affirmations on a daily basis and you'll start believing them!

Some positive affirmations that I find help me:

- I am enough and worthy of love.

- I define my career, my career doesn't define me.

- I don't have to be perfect to be badass.

- I can, I will.

- I'm doing the best I can and that's good enough.

- I'm not perfect but I'm perfectly me.

- My flaws make me unique.

Anxiety

For me, thought loops can cause anxiety. Ruminating about something that's bothering me is one of my worst habits which I've applied kindfulness to in order to change. It takes time and practice, but when you realize that the hours spent playing out scenarios and worrying – especially about something that has not yet happened or might not even occur – are a waste of time, energy and emotion, the quicker you alert yourself to thought loops. I taught myself to use distraction tactics: I'd make myself stop and recognize that I was doing myself no good going over and over a worry; I'd move rooms, find a chore to do, have a chat on the phone or, my number one, listen to music. Music is my greatest weapon against thought loops, especially on long car journeys when I can be sucked down a worry wormhole of my own making while driving alone for three hours.

I don't spend time thinking deeply about something awesome that is happening in my life – but throw a future event my way that I have little or no control over and I'd waste hours – if not days – going over and over it in my mind, playing out scenarios and working out how I'd react to different situations. If I could take my head off and pop it on a shelf to give myself a break from overthinking I totally would. Because my natural need is to solve problems.

Fortunately, I recognize what my anxiety triggers are. It doesn't make the experience any more comfortable, but I don't panic. 'This is anxiety. It's here because I'm stressed. It will pass. Just breathe deeply.' Breathing is at the heart of mindfulness.

Dr Elizabeth Hoge, a psychiatrist at the Center for Anxiety and Traumatic Stress Disorders at Massachusetts General Hospital, and an assistant professor of psychiatry at Harvard Medical School, has spoken about how mindfulness meditation makes perfect sense for treating anxiety because you can train yourself to recognize 'unproductive worries' and negative thoughts.

'People with anxiety... can't distinguish between a problem-solving thought and a nagging worry that has no benefit,' Dr Hoge has said.

'You might think, "I'm late, I might lose my job if I don't get there on time, and it will be a disaster!" Mindfulness teaches you to recognize, "Oh, there's that thought again. I've been here before. But it's just that, a thought, and not a part of my core self".'

Why mindfulness is for you

Camilla Sacre-Dallerup, life coach, hypnotherapist and bestselling author of *Reinvent Me*, says...

I've come to prioritize being kind to myself over many things in life, simply because when I take care of myself it improves not just my own life but those of the people around me, too. I simply have to practise mindfulness and meditate daily to be able to feel happier and more confident. Over years of practising mindfulness and meditation myself – and seeing the positive changes my clients have made through using it daily – I've seen that doing a short meditation can change your day. And, making it a daily practice, it can change your life. What is so magical about practising mindfulness and meditation is that we can just go for a walk or close our eyes. Simply say to yourself, 'I'm taking this moment to be kind to myself and I acknowledge the feeling of xyz.'

Breathe

As you connect to your breath, those issues, feelings or emotions lose their grip. There really is huge power in surrendering to the breath and taking a moment to allow ourselves to just be. When we get caught up in our thinking, it's easy to get stuck believing there is no way out. But when you have made friends with meditation, you know you have a mindful tool up your sleeve ready to be used anytime you need it. Choosing to be kind to yourself is pure nurture for your soul.

Put yourself first

If you please everyone except yourself, you can become depleted. It's our job to look after ourselves first. Learn to say no. Way too often we say yes to things when we really want to say no. We end up sacrificing our own happiness in order to please others. Scheduling in sufficient downtime and sleep time is vital. A really beautiful way to look after ourselves is to say: 'I take this time for me because I respect myself, my body and my mind.' It's pure kindness.

Listen to your body

I spent way too many years pushing myself as a professional dancer, only to find myself exhausted and burnt out. It's a long climb up from there, so listen to your body's signals before it's too late.

The body is really good at telling us when we need to rest and when we need to take time to have fun. Our intuition is a magical thing that will bring us great happiness if we allow it to guide us.

Find your happy

Choosing to be kind to ourselves is a conscious choice we can make each day. Spend time in solitude – a walk or a hot bath – where you can just allow the thoughts to flow in and out of your mind. Allow your thoughts to simply pass through like clouds in the sky. I schedule these nurture highlights into my week, to make sure I have the time.

The kindfulness mantra

One of the kindest things you can do is to remind yourself daily: 'I am enough, I love and validate myself fully.'

Even if you don't truly believe the words at first, the more you say them the truer they will become to you.

Dating & relationships

I'm single, so will the 'smug marrieds' scoff at my words of relationship wisdom as I navigate the dating scene?

But this isn't just about romantic love. It's about every kind of love – parents, siblings, friendships, and everything in between. About falling out of love and ending toxic friendships. And building connections when family relations are strained. Because you deserve to be happy and loved unconditionally. And you've got the power to make sure that happens.

Happily single

Most people think happily single is an oxymoron.

'Ah you've just not found the right man yet.' Or he hasn't found me.

'Don't you get lonely?' No, actually, I don't.

'Oh, you're a career woman.' Well…

When that last statement was chucked in my direction, I set him straight. 'You wouldn't say that to a guy would you? And no one asks, "Why are career men putting off fatherhood?" Having a career is not a reason to be single. Not meeting the right person is.'

It's taken me a long time to be able to say with absolute certainty that I'm enough. I'm worthy of love. And deserving of it. There's a reason why the saying, 'You have to love yourself before you love someone else' gets bandied around a lot.

I look back at my younger self and want to shake her and hug her at the same time for all the wasted time when she lacked confidence and wasn't kind enough to herself. Now, when I have a moment of self-doubt, I catch myself and reframe the thought.

'He won't be interested in me' becomes, 'If he's not interested in me then he's missing out.'

'He doesn't fancy me' becomes, 'If he doesn't fancy me that doesn't mean I'm unattractive.'

By being kinder to myself, I'm open to dating – but these days I'm auditioning guys rather than waiting to see if they like me. I'm not going to be everyone's cup of tea, and that's OK. But I finally have the confidence to know that I'm a catch and someone would be lucky to date me.

I recently went for a drink with a guy I like. A couple of years ago the date would have been doomed before I even took the first sip of my G&T. I would have had anxiety for days before, ruminating over every possible outcome, obsessing over how the night would play out and trying to work out if he liked me. I'd ruin any possibility of a relationship by becoming an angst-ridden version of myself, pre-empting what he wanted to hear rather than presenting the best version of myself and seeing if we were a good match – and, more importantly, if he had enough to offer me to keep me interested.

Oh, Taylor Swift circa 2012 had nothing on me. Dating was more a practice of self-hating.

I'd screw up – proving I wasn't worth dating in the first place.

I was self-sabotaging my love life for two reasons: I didn't love myself so I didn't have the core belief that I was worthy of love. And I couldn't handle anyone being able to impact on my emotional equilibrium.

Single = I was in control of my emotions. Or so I thought.

As soon as I developed feelings for a guy it made me miserable. I was constantly anxious. So I just avoided dating. Or developed a 'safe crush' on a guy who'd friend-zoned me. Repeat to fade...

I was a self-fulfilling prophecy.

But I'm proof you can change. I'm happily single and optimistic about dating and falling in love with an awesome guy. It's nothing less than I deserve. I know that now. Yes, I need to put myself out there more. But I'm working on it.

'The most important relationship in life
is the one you have with yourself.
And if you have that, any other
relationship is a plus and
not a must.'

Diane von Furstenberg

How to date well

TV dating expert **Nadia Essex** says...

Self-confidence is key to a happy relationship. There is nothing more attractive than a man or woman who is comfortable in their own skin.

Learn confidence

There's a difference between feeling a little inse-cure about yourself and feeling so bad that you're not ready to date again.

If you are dating purely to find someone to give you confidence, then you're not likely to find your perfect partner. You'll settle for a partner that isn't right and ultimately another messy break-up. All because you put your happiness in the hands of others.

No one can make you happy. They can make you smile, they can make you laugh but they can-not make you fundamentally happy. You have to take responsibility for your own happiness.

Stop dating!

I tell a lot of my coaching clients to completely

stop dating. Delete all dating apps and take relationships off the table. Then, once they do that, the pressure is off. Being single is healthy. It's a place you can learn about yourself, learn to love yourself and learn how to be the best partner you can be.

Once my clients have stopped focusing on finding a partner, I then tell them to start focusing on themselves. Do something selfish that makes them happy at least once a week.

Within a few weeks they all come back with their confidence levels dramatically increased and they are usually mentally ready to start dating again.

Deal with rejection

We apply for many jobs during our careers where we will be rejected, but won't put ourselves forward for one date for fear of rejection.

The easiest way to avoid rejection is to learn how to read the signals. Unfortunately, online dating has ruined society's flirting skills. I teach all my clients flirting tips to bring it back. All single people should feel confident in flirting and reading signals so initial rejection becomes almost obsolete.

The two things to look out for to see if that person is into you straight away: eye contact and tactile attention.

First-date advice

Date less, date better.

If you're online dating, suggest meeting for a coffee fairly soon into chatting. Coffee is NOT a date. Coffee is a meeting to see if you have chemistry. If you have chemistry then the next meet is the date.

Let the man ask you out. Men usually give no mixed signals. If they like you they will message back almost straight away. If they are into you they will ask to meet up, and if they want a second date you will know within 48 hours of the first date.

Give him a chance to see how much he is into you – then you can make a decision on whether you want to go out again. If the guy you are dating isn't doing any of these things, he is not that into you.

Next!

Being selfish in a relationship

It's in our nature to care for others and want to make them happy. And in the early stages of a relationship we're likely to be flexible, adapting ourselves into a couple mould to see how we fit together. But it's sometimes easy to lose your sense of self when you're a couple. And putting our own needs first can end with resentment building up.

So how can we be positively selfish and make sure our own needs are met in a relationship? Communication.

Whenever I hear a friend talking (well, moaning) about their partner, the first question I ask is, 'Have you talked to them about this?' More often than not it's a 'no'. Or not properly.

It's so easy to blame your partner for a breakdown in communication when times are tough. But if you're in a relationship, you're still responsible for your own happiness. Just because someone loves you, you shouldn't rely on them to feed your happiness or self-confidence.

In a healthy relationship, two people bring two full cups with them (water, coffee, gin – whatever works for you!). When one cup is knocked over by the stress of life or ends up half empty, your cup can help top it up. You're responsible for keeping your own cups full. So you can always rely on each other. But if you don't take care of your own cup and rely on your partner's, you're never able to top theirs up, which can lead to resentment and you becoming dependent on them and their need to keep you full. Which isn't a healthy balance for any relationship.

Taking care of yourself and your own happiness is essential. Being positively selfish and being able to communicate your needs is a must. Know your self-worth and make sure your partner does too. Ultimately, if your partner doesn't treat you in the way you deserve – with respect, loyalty, time, love and honesty – then you need to decide if you want to be in that relationship.

When a friend would tell me about the toxic relationship she felt trapped in, I would keep asking what advice she would have for me if I was describing how unhappy I was and how badly I was being treated. She agreed she'd tell me to end it. It took her a long time but she left that relationship and is happier than ever building her self-confidence back up.

We should always treat ourselves like we do our best friends. You deserve happiness.

Tom Read Wilson from TV's *Celebs Go Dating* says:

My core advice to all daters is deceptively simple: Celebrate you – warts and all! This applies to the first date and to the 75th in equal measure.

Your soulmate, curiously, will fall harder for creases in the silk than the silk itself. It seems mind-boggling to the owner since we're always trying to iron them out, but it's true! After all, what is it you discover/rediscover when sitting face to face on a date? I think the most important answer is idiosyncrasies.

These little flashes of nuanced behaviour are not (as many believe) the arsenal of foibles that prevent one being loveable. They are the very thing that makes one delicious. These traits and quirks are the charming details that are lost in the day-to-day and come flooding back over a candlelit meal for two. And if you're embarking on a first date, celebrate them then, too! They make you you.

This notion will liberate you utterly. And, of course, the scrumptious by-product of that is that this ease in your own skin makes you irresistible. It also encourages a kind of transparency and candour that serves the relationship terribly well. Go forth and be you – uncensored, unedited, undiluted!

46% of people who took the kindfulness survey said they put themselves last on their family priority list.

It's good to talk

No one wants to feel like they are being taken for granted. Unfortunately, you don't become a mind reader when you fall in love. If you want something – emotionally, sexually or simply just for dinner! – you have to communicate. You're equally responsible for making the relationship work. So make sure your needs are met by talking. Put time in your diaries if you have to – date night anyone? – and talk about the good things you've done together and the bumps you've been through. Don't blame or belittle. But if mistakes have been made, suggest you learn from them. 'Next time can you…?'

Women often take on the role of present-buyer for the whole family – including their partner's. And then complain about it. You're making the choice to do it. You're in control. If you don't enjoy it, discuss it with your partner.

I think a relationship is a bit like a doubles tennis partnership:

You're working together as a team with the same ambition.

You both try to cover the other when there's a difficult shot lobbed in your direction.

One of you might stumble but the other is always ready to step in to help.

You constantly communicate your needs, congratulate each other on your wins and both try harder if one of you misses a shot.

It's exhausting and frustrating at times.

Swearing and racquet-throwing only get you in trouble.

But if you try your best and work together you'll be winners.

Love all.

Kindfulness survey

You say...

What makes you happiest in your relationship?

◆ 'Spending time together.'

◆ 'Sex.'

◆ 'Feeling appreciated and looked after.'

◆ 'When we laugh together.'

◆ 'Having found my favourite person.'

◆ 'Contentment. Confidence. Great sex and loving moments.'

◆ 'Time alone with my wife without the kids is bliss.'

◆ 'Good sex, a strong connection in terms of shared values, interests, ethics and humour.'

◆ 'Feeling loved and respected.'

◆ 'Just spending time together outside walking.'

◆ 'Understanding and appreciation.'

◆ 'Having someone who thinks you're the bee's knees, and tells you every day in a reassuring way. You're completely a team together, so there's nothing you have to face on your own.'

Couples coach and sex expert **Annabelle Knight** gives her advice on applying kindfulness to your relationship...

The word 'selfish' is hardly ever used positively and yet it can really help to enhance your relationship.

Compromising on your happiness should never be an option and certainly isn't conducive to a healthy and well-balanced relationship – which is why being positively selfish is a good thing. Knowing your true self and not compromising on that is the only way to be truly happy in a relationship, otherwise your generosity and actions of perceived selflessness become more of a transaction, in a sort of tit-for-tat way.

If you are true to yourself, everything becomes easier: communication flows more naturally and the relationship becomes stronger, as the love that you give and receive is based on nothing but honest actions and emotions.

If you aren't happy in your relationship then you need to ask yourself why, and be honest about it. Once you have pinpointed the reason, talk to your partner, be concise and respectful and listen intently to their reply so that you can move forward together.

One of the most common problems I come across is one partner feeling emotionally neglected, which can leak into other areas of the relationship. This is where great communication and, sometimes, being a little selfish comes in handy.

It's so important to remember that you are an individual as well as part of a couple. Take time to do things that make you feel good on a personal level: exercise, socializing or a hobby. Taking care of yourself and ensuring you are happy and healthy both physically and mentally will have a positive effect on you and your relationship.

Give your relationship an MOT

What are the five things that matter to you most in a relationship? Do you have them?

Identify any areas that you need work on – should you make more time to talk together and plan your future, or are you stuck in a rut of competitive stress? What are the things you love to do together – when was the last time you did them? Can you schedule in time to do them more often? Is there anything you want your partner to do more of – or less?

Sit down with your partner and write down 10

things you love about each other and what you'd like to thank them for. Swap and then read them out loud. Showing appreciation for each other can start a much-needed conversation about your relationship and what you want to get out of it.

Managing difficult family relationships

There may be people in your life who are not easy to walk away from but don't make you happy – a sibling, in-law or your own parents.

If there's someone in your family you have a difficult relationship with, you are not alone. Families are complex and can be dysfunctional. Everyone feels pressure to have the perfect family set-up but that's just not the case for many people. Throw emotions into the mix, and managing difficult family relationships can be tough.

Remember the following...

- It doesn't matter if someone is related to you, they have no right to speak to you rudely or treat you disrespectfully.

- Stay calm. If they push your buttons, take a breath before responding.

- You're not going to be able to change a narcissist even if you share some DNA.

And a relative who is permanently
pessimistic won't change their outlook
just because you're the same blood
type.

◆ Kill them with kindness. Smile your
response and it can be disarming. When
disagreeing, do so with a steady tone
and change the subject. Counting to
10 and breathing deeply works too.

◆ You are an adult. And you should be
treated like one. Set boundaries. Make
sure you act like an adult – slipping
back into childhood habits or behaviour
sends out the wrong signals. Exert your
confidence.

◆ Some people are just negative by nature.
Avoid getting pulled into their drama.
Remove yourself from their company,
use the 'it's nothing to do with me' card
and change the subject.

- Just because you're blood-related doesn't mean you have anything in common. I have friends who are nothing like their family and choose not to spend time with them. Be you. And if the best version of you means not being around family members, that's OK. It doesn't make you a bad person. It means you're putting yourself first. And that's what kindfulness is all about.

Friendships

I don't know where I'd be without my best friends. I have a Heroes box of mates from school, university, work, and some I've just picked up along the way. Some I've known for over 30 years and others I've made more recently.

We connect with people over common interests and passions. And, over the years, as we change and grow, our friendships do too. It can be difficult to accept that a friendship has changed. When you care about someone and they don't feel the same way, you naturally feel rejected. And the end of a friendship can be as difficult to accept as a relationship breakdown.

Ultimately, we deserve to surround ourselves with cheerleaders, with people who support us, believe in us and are there in the good times and the bad. I think people fall into two categories: drains and radiators – they either suck us of energy and emotion or radiate warmth and love.

When I came to looking at how kindfulness applies to my friendships, I recognized a pattern of behaviour. I had always thought it was a good trait to be adaptable within my friendships – if they were an alpha mate, I'd take a back seat; if they were more laid-back, I'd step into an alpha role and lead. It seemed like the natural thing to do to keep my friends happy.

But I was doing myself a disservice. I would often not speak up about what I wanted to do and was silently frustrated. That wasn't my friends' fault – it was mine for not taking responsibility for my own happiness and communicating my needs. Again, my people-pleaser tendencies were in full force and it needed to change.

Looking back, there have been moments in which I've been kindfully kick-ass. When I had a long-term friend screaming in my face, I said we needed to take some time out. It was like a break-up and I missed her terribly. But she was projecting her own issues onto me and I'm worth more than being someone's punch bag. We're still in touch but I know I deserve to be treated better than that, and she respects me more for it.

Know your worth. If a friend belittles you, puts you down in front of other people, hijacks conversations when you're mid-flow, regularly cancels on you and doesn't give you the time you deserve, it's OK to step away. Take time out. Or break up with them.

Since applying kindfulness to my friendships, I get more out of them and have become more aware of my own shortcomings – I speak up instead of expecting mates to know what I want. And I only spend time with people who make me feel great about myself. I make the most of my time with my friends. I've found friendships have to be reinvented when kids come along. Allowances have to be made. Effort put in on both sides. The friendship between parents and non-parents can be fraught as you find a new way of spending time together with little ones in tow. But, in my experience, it's worth being patient and finding a new way to carve out your friendship.

'Don't let the noise of others' opinions drown out your inner voice.'

Steve Jobs

Kindfulness rules for friendship

Accept friendships change

There's a natural ebb and flow to friendships – life can get in the way, whether it's distance, marriage, children or work. Decide whether you want to make that extra effort or let the friendship fade. Just like relationships, friendships often have a life span, and that's OK. People come into our lives for different reasons and for varying amounts of time. Know that, and you'll be able to accept changes easier.

Set boundaries

When you're on a night out, please put your phone away. It's one of my biggest bugbears. I consciously avoid keeping my phone on the table – if I do, it's turned screen-side down. I've asked mates to put their phones away if they keep checking messages. For me, it implies they are not invested in spending quality time with you. And you deserve to have a friend's full attention, don't you?

Cull toxic friends

Your time is precious. Don't waste it with anyone who makes you feel crap. You don't have to agree with your friends all the time, but respect is part of friendship. If someone stresses you out, stop spending time with them. I'm not talking about people going through problems, but the negative Nancys and Nigels who never have a good word to say about anything or anyone. Give yourself permission to be fussy about friends. Life is too short to hang out with anyone who doesn't make us feel like we're important to them. If you get a whiff of toxicity about a friend, have a conversation, be up front about their behaviour and explain that it upsets you. And if they don't take that on board and show some respect, don't spend time with them. It's that simple. If a friend continues to disappoint you, walk away. If they're self-centred there'll be no room for you in their life and you deserve a friend's full attention and love. As the saying goes, 'Real queens fix each other's crowns'.

Find your tribe

Surround yourself with cheerleaders. Everyone goes through tough times and you'll have to be there for them, too. But having a handful of people you can rely on to be there in tough times is a must. Invest time and effort into your friendships and expect to get the same out of them. Find the men and women who celebrate your success, encourage you to follow your dreams and pick you up when you fall. Celebrate success together and be there to pick each other up. Good friendships are worth investing in.

You are in control of your friendships

Don't put up with someone treating you badly and just moan about it to other friends. It's your fault if you stick with a toxic friend. You cannot change other people. You CAN set boundaries that can have a positive effect. But do not be a mate martyr. It will only make you miserable in the long term. If someone is going through a tough time – experiencing mental health issues or relationship difficulties – you can't fix their problems for them. You can arm them with information about organizations that can help and encourage them to seek help. Give them the power to help themselves. But ultimately they have to want to help themselves.

'Friendship goals, not own goals,' – me!

Kindfulness survey

You say...
Have you ever cut out a toxic friend?

- 'They made me feel guilty for not feeling the same about them as they did for me. I sent them a long text message explaining.'

- 'I've let friendships with hyper-negative people end. I stopped making an effort to spend time with them and didn't validate their negative focus.'

- 'They were transferring their stresses onto me and were takers. I started saying no and drew lines. They didn't like it and stopped talking to me. From then on, I didn't let others dictate my choices.'

- 'I often do this. You should only be surrounded by friends who uplift you.'

- 'They were angry when drinking and in general. They didn't bring me any happiness or have qualities I look for so I cut them out.'

- 'I let us drift apart so that the friendship fizzled out. She was quite princess-like and I felt I had to walk on eggshells round her. She had the power to hurt me.'

- 'I don't do toxic vampires – they were depressing, self-absorbed and drama queens.'

- 'She became a taker and my emotional bank account ran dry with her around.'

- 'Negative and jealous. We stopped talking when she told me to shut up talking at a dinner party.'

8

Parenting

One of the biggest conversations I have with my parent friends is about guilt and worry. Of course, mums and dads are going to worry about their kids. But it should never get to a point when it's impacting negatively on the parent's self-worth.

For the majority of parents, putting their own needs first doesn't come easily – so being positively selfish can be a struggle. There is little time for a mum and dad to have any 'me time' and often just the thought of it is enough to kick off a guilt trip.

No matter what happens in a day – tantrums,

meals pushed away, screens banned – when you tuck your kids up at night you've already won. You got through another day and kept a small person alive. You're doing the best job you can and should take a moment to congratulate yourself instead of being self-critical and feeling guilty about what you haven't done. I am in awe of you all.

Some parents admit they've lost their sense of self when they've taken on the role of mum or dad. And while they're never going to be the same person again (understatement!), I believe making time for themselves and taking care of their own needs makes them a happier and better parent in the long-term.

Yes, it might mean tag-teaming with your partner or calling in babysitting favours from friends or family, but it's worth scheduling in some time for yourself. Because parents deserve kindfulness in bucketloads. Whether it's a long bath in absolute silence, time to work out at the gym, a 10-minute walk, a concert or cinema trip *sans* kids, YOU deserve some time to yourself. It's not selfish to feed your own passions.

Who are your tribe that would love to spend

time with your kids – friends, godparents, aunts and uncles? Talk to them about spending time with the children and plan some exciting days out.

I relish the time I spend with my niece, nephew and godchildren, and gladly step in for play dates to give my sister some time to herself. Many of my child-free friends are more than happy to help out with their mates' children and are just waiting to be asked. It gives us non-parents time to bond with your children, who we love.

So stop feeling guilty about 'palming your children off' onto someone else and look at it this way – child-free friends LOVE your children and would like the chance to run around the local park or the excuse to see the new Pixar movie. Our hands are free and ready to hold your children's. Just call us and go enjoy some quality time with your partner, read a book, go shopping or have a lie down. Naps aren't just for toddlers!

Kindfulness survey

You say...
What do you feel guilty about?

- 'I don't do enough. I'm not trying my best. I'm not good enough.'

- 'I'm struggling to achieve work/family balance and someone or something is always missing out.'

- 'Guilty that I work full-time so don't spend enough time with them. I don't make enough memories with them. I shout too much. I'm not consistent enough because I don't have the energy.'

- 'Not being a good enough mum.'

- 'Not spending time with the children, and finding their games boring. Not spending enough time on their schoolwork.'

- 'I sometimes feel guilty for not wanting to be a parent all the time.'

- 'Not being a calm, laid-back parent.'

- 'Working and not being good at playing. I feel intolerant to whining.'

- 'Not doing enough things for my children. Wanting time on my own.'

- 'Am I doing it right? Leaving baby with grandparents when I go back to work. Not getting out of the house enough.'

- 'I'm too busy to give my kids a lot of my time and sometimes I shout when we're having a bad day.'

- 'I have stepchildren so the relationship is one of constant guilt – not approachable enough, too approachable, doormat, not strict enough, too strict.'

- 'Being at work and paying someone to look after them when it should be me.'

- 'Being a bad parent or feeling resentful that you have put your own life on hold for the benefit of your children.'

- 'When I'm working I feel I should be doing things with the kids, and when I'm with the kids I feel bad that I have work to do.'

- 'Shouting. Not being there enough. Giving him too much screen time.'

- 'I feel guilty that my little boy isn't spending enough time with other kids – we've just moved abroad and we live in a rural part of France. I feel guilty that I'm not playing with him enough, but also that I'm smothering him!'

Kindfulness for mums and dads

Anna Williamson, NLP life coach, mum-of-one and author of *Breaking Mum and Dad*, says...

Make yourself a priority

I always say you have to put yourself first before you can be the best you can be to everyone else... and, yes, that does include your kids!

Our children are of course precious and of the highest importance, but running ourselves ragged emotionally, physically and mentally isn't going to help anyone, least of all your kids. So it's hugely important to be kind to yourself every day and make time for YOU time... even just using the loo in peace can help in not feeling so frazzled.

Dealing with guilt

Parenting guilt is something every parent feels, and it's such a wasted emotion at times. But the good news is, it means we care!

Instead of letting guilt make you feel bad, as though you're not doing things right, embrace the fact that you obviously care about your little ones and that makes you a great parent. Put guilt to one side and congratulate yourself on all you ARE doing, not what you're not.

Couple time

Relationships often end up at the bottom of the pile of priorities when you throw children into the mix. It might sound a bit forced, but it's important to set aside time for each other, and spend time without the children to keep your interests and emotional bond strong. Don't feel guilty about using babysitters every now and again – it's important for your own well-being.

There's no such thing as a perfect parent

Without a doubt, sleep deprivation and juggling work life and family are the most talked about issues to do with parenting that I come across on a daily basis. We have to remember that we don't have to be perfect, in fact nobody is ever perfect – particularly when it comes to being a mum or dad.

Take each day as it comes; some days will be great, some days will be not so great, and that is OK. Just recognizing how you are feeling, doing what you feel able to, and not putting pressure on yourself can go a long way in reducing any negativity.

Ditch the guilt

Ask your friends and family to describe you as a parent and write it down as a list. Look at the words they use – that's the kind of mum or dad you are. When you're doubting yourself as a parent, look at your list and read the words out loud.

Me time

Write a list of all the things you'd do if you had 10 minutes to yourself. Can you fit a few of them into your week? What if you had a free hour? And what if you had a full child-free day or weekend?

Whether you're a single parent or part of a couple, having some time to yourself is rare. Do you have family or friends who would jump at the chance to spend time with your kids? Book them in for a few weekends over the next six months and make the most of your child-free days – going away is optional but a lie-in is a must!

9

Your body

The UK government did research ('The part played by poor body image in our physiological and psychological well-being, on our confidence and aspirations') back in 2015 and launched a body confidence campaign. Why? Because feeling crap about our bodies is holding us back in life.

Experts had evidence to suggest that people with poor body image are more likely to lack self-esteem, making them vulnerable to peer and partner pressure: 'They are also more likely to be depressed and may return to risky coping strategies and self-soothing behaviours. These can include risky behaviours such as not taking care of themselves during sex, vomiting or purging, alcohol and drug abuse, crash-dieting, smoking to control appetite, and self-harm.'

And, according to the report, nearly half of all adults (47%) think that 'how you look affects what you can achieve in life', and around one-third (32%) agree with the statement 'your value as a person depends on how you look'.

If half of us think how we look affects what we can achieve in life and a third think our looks equate to our value as a person, anyone with poor body image is probably settling for what they can get rather than striving to be the best they can.

Society clearly projects the notion that 'attractiveness' (which has to be in quotation marks because I'm assuming we'll go by whatever the fashion/beauty industry and media has decided is the 'right' look at the moment) = value.

I call bullshit. And so do you.

According to another survey, 9 out of 10 adults would like to see a broader range of body shapes shown in advertising and the media.

The Expert Advisory Group have also flagged

the negative impact the media is having on our body image, saying: 'There is widespread public concern about the effects of the ways women are portrayed in the media – in particular, about the limited range of ways in which women are portrayed, about sexualization, about the invisibility of women who are not young, white, heterosexual and conventionally beautiful.'

Learning to love my body

I've rarely been kind or mindful towards my body. Indifferent. Ashamed of being plus-size, perhaps. Because in our society, skinny = sexy and plus-size = lazy. I started working on my relationship with my body with one rule in mind: be kinder.

Now, you might have a great relationship with yours. Friends of mine hit the gym regularly, get lots of fresh air, drink in moderation, eat well with the occasional treat. They are living their best lives when it comes to their physical self.

But for many of us, it's a struggle. And when we do consider our bodies, we can't see how wonderful they are without being distracted by the so-called flaws and imperfections we've been conditioned to hate/be ashamed of.

I have...

- ◆ cellulite
- ◆ spots
- ◆ lumps
- ◆ bumps
- ◆ love handles
- ◆ bra bulge
- ◆ double chin
- ◆ the occasional hair growing out of aforementioned chin
- ◆ too much hair on my top lip
- ◆ hairy big toes
- ◆ scars from my appendix operation
- ◆ a belly
- ◆ short fingers
- ◆ not white-enough teeth

You get the drift.

But I'm over beating myself up about this list. I'm keen to lose weight so I'm healthier and fitter. And the side effect of this will be less belly and more energy. But, as for the rest... I can pluck that dark, wiry chin hair and shave my toes. Plus, there are parts of my body that I genuinely love.

My question to you – is there anything you would like to change about your body? And do you have the ability to change it?

If it makes you happier to be 10lb heavier or 10lb lighter, go for it. But are you truly happy when you reach that goal weight? If you're plucked, waxed, whipped into shape by a personal trainer, have a dazzling Hollywood smile that would put Simon Cowell to shame, and not an inch of cellulite because you've spent hundreds on treatments – are you happier? Or will you find another flaw to fix? Or another 5lb to lose?

It took me a long time to realize that accepting your body as it is – right now – is a big deal. Learning to love every lump and bump doesn't come easily when we're bombarded by images of celebrities who, let's face it, don't look like the average man or woman.

But I've come to one conclusion – accepting your body, your shape, your size, your flaws and your beauty helps you to be kinder to it. I appreciate my body for being able to walk for miles, run around after my niece and nephew and dance like no one is watching – although my friends often are watching and videoing me for lols.

I don't know what size I'll end up. That is irrelevant, quite frankly – as is the number on the scales.

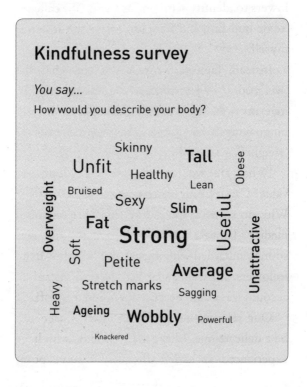

Kindfulness survey

You say...
How would you describe your body?

Skinny

Tall

Unfit

Healthy

Obese

Lean

Bruised

Overweight

Sexy

Slim

Fat

Strong

Useful

Soft

Unattractive

Petite

Average

Heavy

Stretch marks

Sagging

Ageing

Wobbly

Powerful

Knackered

Weight is just a number

In early 2018, TV presenter and star of hit US show *The Good Place*, Jameela Jamil, caused a social media storm when she challenged an Instagram post which had the Kardashians' weights written on each woman and invited followers to identify with one of them. She called it 'toxic bullshit', and I couldn't have put it better myself.

Instead, Jameela wrote a post of what she 'weighed' ('lovely relationship, great friends, love my job, financially independent, like my bingo wings'), and asked followers to share their 'weights'.

'What are we teaching women about our value? Can it be measured using a metric system? Why do so many posts like this exist on social media?' Jameela wrote on her blog, and was soon bombarded with images and 'weights' from followers. She went so far as to start an Instagram account @i_weigh because the trend took off.

Our relationship with our body image can be a delicate one. I have many friends who have experienced an eating disorder at some point in their lives. And some of my friends – of all shapes and sizes – are not as body confident as they should be.

The media are obsessed with weight. Especially women's. I'm yet to see an article comparing the waist measurements of Brad Pitt, Kanye West, Chris Hemsworth, Michael B. Jordan and Channing Tatum.

I'm certainly not dismissing men's body image issues. In recent years, the number of adult men being admitted to hospital with an eating disorder has risen by 70% – the same rate of increase as women. And if you're worried that you or someone you love might be experiencing an eating disorder, there are organizations that can help on pages 191–3.

You are enough. You are perfectly you. You are capable of any positive change you want to make. But you are already enough.

> 90% of people who took the kindfulness survey believe celebrity culture impacts on the way we feel about our bodies.

Learning to love my body after an eating disorder

Gemma Oaten, actress and patron of eating disorder support service, SEED, says...

I developed anorexia aged just 10. By the age of 11 I was given 24 hours to live and admitted to a children's psychiatric unit. I demolished my body because I thought it would stop the pain inflicted on me by bullies. It didn't. I nearly died three times over the next 12 years, but began recovery aged 23.

Now, at 34, I'm a successful actress, charity campaigner and patron of eating disorder support service, SEED, which was set up by my wonderful mum and dad.

What I've learnt...

No one is perfect

No one is 'normal' – who defines normal anyway?! We're all unique. We're all special in so many beautiful and individual ways. You are selling yourself short if you compare yourself to others. Physically and mentally.

Your self-worth comes from within

One thing I know is being kind to your body is the greatest gift you can ever give yourself. Ultimately, it is the gift of life.

Fuel your body in the right way

I used to be addicted to exercise and starve my body. I now work out regularly and make sure I eat in the right way. Every mouthful and gym session makes me mindful that I am CHOOSING to be kind to ME.

Be the change you want to see

I treat my body like a flower... keeping it watered and fed so it grows and blooms. And, as I always say, you can always grow flowers where dirt used to be.

The kindfulness diet plan

Since deciding to stop beating myself up for being 'fat, lazy and unattractive' (I mean, bloody hell, we can be so mean to ourselves, can't we?), I've started losing weight. I deserve to treat myself like I'm already beautiful. That would be the kind thing to do, right?

Once I decided to be kindful to my body, I started making changes. This is what I did:

Didn't go on a diet

That's the kindfulness diet plan: don't go on a diet. Instead, I started being more mindful about what I was eating. Nothing was off limits. But when you start being kind to your body, you want to treat it nicely. That meant more fruit and vegetables. All the stuff we know we're supposed to do until that bar of chocolate/slice of pizza/piece of cake ends up in our hands. All I did was keep track of what I was eating a bit more. I still treated myself to cheesecake, but didn't go overboard. If I had a blow-out meal, I didn't beat myself up. I started a fresh the next day. It certainly didn't feel like a diet. That was a big thing for me – you can't fail at something you're not doing. Every day I did my best to treat my body well. And that was enough.

Stopped making excuses

If you're overweight, you're eating too much and not moving around enough (unless you have a health issue, which the majority of overweight people don't). I'm the only person responsible for putting food and drink in my mouth and moving my body. So I put more thought into what I was doing and started taking care of myself.

Stopped stressing

Stress can not only lead to weight gain but can make it more difficult to lose weight. When we're stressed, our bodies are flooded with cortisol, which has been shown to increase the appetite. So it's no wonder so many of us find ourselves mindlessly comfort eating after a hard day at work or during relationship issues. Mindfulness helps you de-stress and builds a better relationship with your body. I try to use apps such as Headspace or Calm for meditation when I can. I should do it more often because I always feel great afterwards.

According to the World Health Organization, stress has been called the 'health epidemic of the twenty-first century', with 10.4 million working days lost each year due to work-related stress.

A YouGov survey revealed that one in five 25- to 34-year-olds are unhappy with their work-life balance. And one in six 45- to 54-year-olds feels the same way. When it comes to working outside their normal hours, two out of five 25- to 34-year-olds believe it's something their employer expects of them.

It's not really surprising, as so many of us strive to 'have it all'. When life feels overwhelming, give yourself a break! You're doing the best you can.

Moving more

I've never been a gym bunny. I doubt I ever will be. I explored acupuncture as another form of self-care and found it gave me energy to want to be more active. I started sleeping better (more on this later) and waking up earlier. And, finally,

I started making more effort to move my body. We all know we need to exercise. But instead of thinking of it as chore, think of it as a treat. The thought of working out gives me a sense of dread and failure, but putting a positive spin on it and believing it's a feel-good treat helps motivate me to get outside for a walk or to do a YouTube yoga workout.

Cutting back on alcohol

After a boozy New Year in Antwerp with friends, I thought I'd give my liver a rest for a week. Which turned into two. Then I thought I'd see if I could do three. And made it to a whole month. It was easier than I thought it would be because I took it a day at a time and booze wasn't banned. I just wasn't drinking. A couple of weeks into my 'non-booze ban' I started reading *The Unexpected Joy of Being Sober* by Catherine Gray – more from her later in this chapter! And it was an eye-opener. For over two decades I'd associated alcohol with celebrating, having a good time, dancing, cheering myself up, commiserating, relaxing. There was a bottle for every occasion, and I'd probably drunk it. Although I never had a drinking problem – and am a good, fun drunk who gets friends home safely, tidies up and makes cups of tea at 4 a.m. – like so many of us I drank way more than the recommended 14 units a week. And I wasn't doing myself any favours by doing so – empty calories, empty purse and empty pack of headache tablets. But at the beginning of the year, I made the decision to cut back for a few days and it's lasted a lot longer. No one is stopping me from drinking. I'm just choosing not to the majority of the time.

Even on 1 February, I was cautious so took it easy with a few drinks. I ended up only having alcohol on one other evening that month.

I went from drinking wine or gin most nights – out with friends or a couple of glasses of red at home to relax – to having a couple of drinks a month. Alcohol was no longer something I relied on to comfort myself with after a busy day, or necessary to celebrate with. It's not banned, but I've disassociated booze with having a good time. I just don't see it as a treat or pick-me-up anymore.

Friends and family were shocked to say the

least – I've yet to find a form of alcohol I don't like! But they soon got used to more sober nights out with me. I'll happily be designated driver. Or simply flag I'm not going to be drinking so we go for an early dinner and they are still welcome to enjoy a glass or three. As far as I'm concerned, if someone has a problem with me not drinking, it's their problem not mine.

A few months after I made the decision to radically cut back, I've enjoyed the odd evening out with a couple of glasses of wine or indulged in a few cocktails, but I'm yet to have a sip of booze at home. Bottles of champagne, wine and gin remain untouched. Instead, I stick to tea, coffee and elderflower cordial or low-sugar squash. I've changed a huge habit in my life and am better off for it. My body is reaping the benefits. My eyes are clearer, my skin brighter and I wake up easier. Zero hangovers and more money in the bank. In my experience, there are NO downsides to cutting down on alcohol.

I'm still a work in progress. I'm still trying to be kind to myself – mind and body. I might not be perfect but I'm perfectly me.

Making sober sexy

Catherine Gray, author of *The Unexpected Joy Of Being Sober*, says...

Before I quit drinking in 2013, I was treating my body with all of the kindfulness of a rock star trashing a hotel room. I was giving it seven or eight bottles of wine a week, 40 menthol cigarettes, a chronic lack of sleep, and could-be-chicken and chips at 1 a.m.

I was caught in a body-bashing cycle. We're told over and over that alcohol is relief, alcohol is relaxation, alcohol is fun, and a small amount is good for you (it's not, by the way) – we don't think of booze as being self-sabotage.

I think of being sober as a radical kindfulness and self-care. Now that I don't drink, it's had a ripple effect on every aspect of my body. I never get fined for skipping yoga, I rarely get less than eight hours sleep a night, I literally have not been to Chicken Cottage in five+ years, and quitting smoking was an absolute doddle once I'd quit drinking.

When I say no to a night out – I never say yes to more than four a week – I think of it as putting my own oxygen mask on first. When I don't take care of my body and don't set boundaries I get ratty, snappy and depressed. So I'm doing everyone a favour by maintaining myself and making sure I get what I need. I never skip my five-times-weekly exercise because exercise is how I decompress and, if I don't do it, I feel like a pressure cooker filled with anxiety.

Psychologically, I make sure my self-esteem is topped up regularly, to challenge the 'loser' voice in my head. I used to rely on other people to do this for me, as if I was an inflatable person who needed to be blown up with praise – but now I do it myself. When I feel myself starting to shrink down into a cycle of meanness ('you haven't done enough today, you are rubbish with money, you need to try harder, do more, be better'), I sit down and write myself a pep-talk letter as a friend would, listing all the things I'm doing right, reminding myself how far I've come, and topping up my self-belief. It works.

You only get one body. YOLO for me means treating that body as our most precious possession, rather than clobbering it with late nights, fags, junk food and booze.

'It is so unkind to punish yourself every day for what you ate last night. You wouldn't do that to another person. I wasted energy on dieting and the burden and struggle of it. Now I have more energy because I am not wasting it on negative stuff.'

Oprah Winfrey

Wake up to sleep

I have a confession to make. I've never really been a morning person. I tend to ease into the day and am always a better person after that first cup of tea.

But I realized I'd accepted the label of 'not a morning person' without hesitation. And so decided to change it. I took that negative label and shoved it where the sun doesn't shine. I decided I AM a morning person as long as I get enough sleep.

Sleep. How often do we complain we're not getting enough hours in the night? Or at least good-quality ZZZZZs? And we all know that we're not on our A game at work when we're knackered.

One of the kindest things we can do for ourselves is to get enough sleep. Sleep deprivation can have a huge impact on our mental well-being. According to a study conducted by Meredith Coles and Jacob Nota at Binghamton University, State University of New York, lack of sleep is linked to negative thoughts and the ability to replace them with more positive ones. The research proved sleeping less than eight hours a night is linked to repetitive negative thoughts like those seen in people experiencing anxiety or depression. And disruptive sleep is associated with the difficulty in shifting your attention away from negative information.

In short, lack of sleep is one of the reasons why negative thoughts can stick around in your head longer than they should and impact on your life. Getting enough sleep will give you the energy you need to be kindful to yourself – to be aware of any negative thoughts and break those damaging loop patterns.

Here are some ways that can help you get a better night's sleep:

◆ Ditch the caffeine after 3 p.m. I'm a coffee- and tea-drinking fiend and am still trying to break this habit!

◆ Ban phones from the bedroom – or at least have a rule that once you're in the bedroom it goes on charge and you don't pick it up to scroll through social media or news sites.

- Don't watch TV in your bedroom at night.

- If you're a couple who struggle to sleep, try separate duvets.

- Make meditation part of your bedtime routine.

- Brain goes into overdrive? Keep a notebook by your bed and write down any worries or things you want to remember to do the next day.

> 47% of people who took the kindfulness survey think they are too self-critical of their bodies.

Build your body confidence: take ownership of your body

You're in charge. Love it just as it is – every stretch mark, every inch of cellulite, every lump, bump and jutting bone. You are enough. Some of the people I know with high body confidence have physical impairments, life-limiting diseases or live with scars. They appreciate what their body does for them far more than most healthy people I know.

If you want to make a change, do it with kindness. Do what makes you feel good – exercise should not be seen as a punishment for the body. You shouldn't go to the gym to 'whip' yourself into shape. Find the right type of movement for you and consider it a treat for your body and mind. Just 30 minutes of brisk walking a day can reduce the symptoms of depression by 36%, according to research.

Notice how you regard your body. If you catch yourself slagging off any part of your body, think about why you feel that way. Is your body really a disappointment or has society conditioned you to consider the way you look a failure?

Thank your body. At the end of the day, think about what your body has done for you. Make your goal to build a better relationship with your body, not achieve the 'perfect' one.

Take care of yourself: baths, long showers, massages and beauty treatments. These are all acts of self-love that can relax you, help switch off a busy mind, and give you some time to yourself and make you feel good about your body.

Body confidence MOT

Take 10 minutes to think about your body. Write down your answers...

◆ How do you feel about your body right now?

◆ How can you be kinder to it?

◆ Look at your body with eyes of love – how would your best friend or partner describe your body? That's how you should be regarding yourself.

◆ What will you do in the next week to be kind to your body?

Body confidence mantras
(feel free to add your own!):

◆ My body might not be perfect but it's perfect for me.

◆ My body is strong and capable.

◆ I am so much more than the numbers on a scale.

◆ I am attractive because of my whole self.

◆ My confidence is the most attractive thing.

10

Work

10

Work

According to the Office for National Statistics, the number of hours we spend in the office every week has increased, with the average working week now 31 hours – growing to 33 hours in London.

And those hours may be spent with people you wouldn't choose to spend your time with. With personalities that might clash with yours. You'll meet some of your best friends and may encounter some bullies along the way. You'll be challenged, promoted and maybe even sacked.

My own career has been a rollercoaster. But when the proverbial shit has hit the fan, I've learnt to hold my nerve. It's not easy to prop up your self-confidence when it takes a bashing, but I'm grateful for every setback, challenge and difficult conversation because they've all been lessons and made me the person I am today. Instead of dwelling on every negative experience I've had in the workplace, I've learnt to turn them into a positive.

Yes, there have been periods of frustration. And I had to be kind to myself to get through them by clinging onto my self-belief by the tips of my probably not-manicured nails.

Here's how I've got through the trickiest times of my career…

I define my career, my career doesn't define me

I'm passionate about journalism and storytelling, particularly when I can use it positively and talk about topics such as mental health and inspirational people. For many years I defined myself by my job. I put work before everything else. I was resilient to setbacks, ploughed through promotions and different jobs – but eventually came to a stark realization. During my time in therapy, I unpicked the relationship I had built with my job and accepted it wasn't beneficial to my self-confidence. I invested so much of myself in my job that my emotional well-being took a knock when something at work didn't go well or I wasn't able to develop as quickly or in the direction that I'd like to. Instead of thriving, at times I became resentful. I felt others were in control of my future. But I was wrong.

You might be in the same self-perpetuating situation:

- Someone has left and you'll take on their tasks on top of your own – yep, I'll do that without asking for a pay rise. Can someone work Bank Holiday Monday? No problem, I'll just see what fun my friends got up to on Facebook instead.

- Someone has to leave their family early after Christmas and work New Year's Eve – oh, I'll happily drive 150 miles back and take that shift while gritting my teeth.

♦ And while being a team player will always be high on my list of priorities – teamwork makes the dream work! – becoming a work martyr isn't a good look. Like the poncho I insisted was great in the early Noughties, I didn't wear it well.

In the past, I've been told: 'If you want something done quickly, give it to the busiest person.' And often that was me. Now, I want to make it clear: I'm proud of my work ethic. But I do regret being a work martyr. And I take full responsibility for it. I have a warning to anyone who 'marries' themselves to their job: proceed with caution. It can impact on your mental health and you may end up feeling bitter about the job you actually love.

Unless you're Richard Branson or Sheryl Sandberg, chances are you have a boss. We're led by them, answer to them and our 'job' is to meet their expectations and please them. As I've said, I was the perfect example of a 'people pleaser' (note the past tense! I am more mindful of this behaviour).

But, after many years of trying to be what I imagined the 'perfect employee' should be, I decided I could be a 'positively selfish employee' instead – and, by doing so, ensure I was getting as much out of my career as I was putting in.

It took a long time and lots of jobs to get there, but all the negative experiences I've had during my career have been invaluable lessons. Working with terrible managers who were unsupportive and uninterested taught me how NOT to manage other people. Leaving a job because it just wasn't working out for me or them showed me sometimes you're just not the right fit, but you're perfect for somewhere else. Being rejected from what I thought was my dream job proved I am tenacious in my career and I refused to let it get me down, moving on to a role which allowed me to shine. And those people who were miserable and mean along the way when I was doing my best – well, they're still miserable and mean. Go figure!

So, whatever you're going through at work, remember to be kind to yourself first and foremost.

'Success isn't about how your life looks to others, it's about how it feels to you. I can promise you that you will never be happy plodding through someone else's idea of success.'

Michelle Obama

Kindfulness survey

You say...
What challenges have you experienced in the workplace that have impacted on your mental health or self-esteem?

- ◆ bullying 23%
- ◆ the job itself 20%
- ◆ overworked 20%
- ◆ your boss and management 14%
- ◆ redundancy 5%
- ◆ too much pressure 5%
- ◆ stress 4%
- ◆ lack of support 3%
- ◆ no promotion 3%
- ◆ other 3%

Career life lessons

◆ Follow your gut

Just because you can do something doesn't mean you should. Develop your passions. Find your own USP. And follow your gut. I have made mistakes because I listened to other people and didn't follow my own instincts. Or did what I thought I should be doing instead of listening to my heart. Ultimately, you know what's right for you. And if you're not sure, write down your options with fors and againsts. It helps you work through decision-making, seeing it in black and white.

◆ **Take control**

Often in the workplace decisions are made that impact on us and are out of our control. This can be a stressful time for anyone. From experience, kindfulness is key to coping with this. Recognizing and accepting you don't have full control over your own role helps you move through turbulent times.

If you're being challenged at work, take some time to sit and think about what you can control: your reaction to the situation; your communication with bosses and colleagues; next steps. Write a list of questions you have and ask for a meeting to clarify anything that's not obvious to you. Do it in person, not by email.

Don't panic. Be kind to yourself if you're feeling anxious or stressed. It's a natural reaction to changes or challenges. Let go of what you can't control and concentrate on what you can.

◆ Future-proof your career

Take time to look into how your industry is developing and what you'll need to do to stay ahead of the pack. Never stop learning, ask to go on courses and develop new skills. Go on management courses – managing upwards is just as important as managing people. I'm proof you can teach an old dog new tricks – I adopted the title 'middle-aged millennial'!

◆ Find your people

For every person who knocked my confidence, there was someone else to offer advice and guidance. Seek out a mentor and don't be afraid to ask for advice on how to get to your goal. I've found people are always flattered when you ask them for advice and only too willing to help.

◆ Embrace change

For every door that shuts, another one opens. Sometimes you're just not looking in the right direction.

Always be open to new opportunities and remind yourself that change, however scary it can seem at first, is just an opportunity for something new – which could be even better. If you find yourself panicking, take five minutes out and remind yourself you're fantastic and will get through whatever life throws at you. Then start a plan of action.

◆ Don't compare yourself to others

The workplace can be a competitive environment. But when you find yourself comparing yourself to others, STOP! In the past, I've been disappointed to see friends' careers flying ahead of my own. But I realized I needed to be kind to myself and stopped beating myself up. Someone else's success doesn't equate to your personal failure. Treat yourself with kindness and celebrate achieving your personal goals. Never measure your own accomplishments against someone else's. Be generous and celebrate your friends' and colleagues' successes. Building a network of smart, loyal, successful mates in the same industry as you is one of the best things you can do to develop your career.

◆ Be kind

Always, always be kind to yourself. I've made mistakes at work and experienced that gut-wrenching feeling of dread. But I don't know one person who hasn't messed up. My advice: Try to solve the problem as soon as you can before telling your boss – then you can explain how you've fixed an issue they didn't even know about, or at least suggest how it can be resolved. You're casting yourself as someone with solutions rather than problems. They'll always appreciate honesty and problem-solving skills over panic.

◆ Take 10 minutes

In Sweden, everyone makes time for a 'fika', a Swedish 'coffee and cake break' which is actually so much more. It's part of Swedish culture to take time out, to pause and give the brain a break, and share a drink and something to eat with colleagues or friends. Slow down and introduce 'fika' into your workplace once or twice a day!

◆ Don't go to work when you're sick

I've been told death was the only valid excuse for not turning up to work. They may have been joking, but I'm not so sure. You are entitled to stay at home if you are too sick to work.

◆ Learn to say no

Managing expectations is a key skill. It's OK to say no. If you're already pushed to the max, explain you've got too much on and see if it can be delegated to someone else while thanking them for the opportunity.

Setting boundaries at work is a must. If you're not going to meet a deadline – speak up. Push back. Discuss your workload. You are entitled to manage your workload, and occasionally that means saying no.

◆ Turn your phone off

We're often expected to check work emails out of hours. Sometimes work may text you out of hours too. Of course, matters of urgency have to be dealt with and, depending on your job, there are different levels of expectations.

Turn your notifications off on your work phone. Beeps or vibrations can be a constant reminder of work. So when you're 'switched off', your phone needs to be switched off too.

Choose when you read your work emails and when to reply to them. Discuss the expectation with your boss if you have any concerns.

◆ Set your own agenda

When you have your next performance review, go armed with goals you'd like to achieve and a plan of how to get there. As a manager, I always wanted feedback from staff on what they wanted to get out of their position, find out what motivated them, and encouraged them to push themselves so they had a sense of purpose and pride.

If you work for yourself, give yourself a PDR (Personal Development Review) – what are your goals for the next year, how can you get there, and who can you collaborate with to keep yourself motivated?

◆ **Keep track of your successes**

Make a list of your successes. When you have moments of frustration, it's great to be able to look back over it and see what you have achieved. It's also useful when having meetings to be able to refer to the moments you're most proud of and what you have learnt along the way.

Be kind to yourself and kick ass!

Managing relationships at work

Let's face it, we're not going to get on with everyone we work with. And that's OK. I've made friends for life in various jobs – but also left behind many people who were just not 'my people'. You bond with some people and tolerate others. But there are always a few of the same characters you come across...

Negative Nancy and Nigel

Those two again! There's always someone who wants to have a moan about work or your boss.

'Your career and your life will have starts and stops and zigs and zags. Don't stress out about the white space – the path you can't draw – because therein lies both the surprises and opportunities.'

Sheryl Sandberg

Don't get pulled into office gossip. It all too often comes back to bite you on the arse if anyone is able to say, 'Well, so and so was saying…' Avoid.

The absent boss

You don't feel supported by your manager and rarely get feedback. It's up to you to manage up and book regular meetings to get feedback. It can be frustrating but you're responsible for getting the most out of your job, so take charge of your own development and use their lack of leadership as a lesson on how NOT to be a manager.

The micro-manager

'How's that coming along?' We've all worked with someone who has checked up on us every five minutes – and on occasion taken credit for our ideas and work. Set boundaries. If they keep checking up on you it's most likely because they don't have faith in their own abilities and assume everyone feels the same way. If you are struggling at work, take advantage and lean on them. If you feel micro-managed, suggest having a five-minute catch-up at the end of the day to update them.

The bitch

Man or woman, there's likely to be someone you just don't get on with at work. If they constantly undermine you, keep track of their behaviour and discuss it with your manager, saying you've noticed a negative pattern of behaviour and you'd like to be able to work better for the benefit of the team. In my experience, if you have a problem it's always better to go to any manager with solutions to an issue or ask for advice on how you can solve it. Be proactive. If someone is making life difficult for you at work, it's a reflection on them NOT you. When I've been in this situation, it was upsetting but clearly driven by jealousy and insecurity on their part. You can't change their outlook on life but you can make sure you remain professional. Success is the best revenge!

Kindfulness survey

You say...

What advice do you have when it comes to managing difficult people?

- 'Speak up.'
- 'Be honest.'
- 'Be assertive.'
- 'Communicate.'
- 'Pretend to be Deborah Meadon – she scares me, so it makes me feel like I'm in complete control and helps me exert authority.'
- 'Take time to consider where they are coming from and what they need. And get advice from someone else.'
- 'Think about why they are difficult – is it them or your perception of them? Can you change your behaviour towards them?'
- 'Ask for advice.'
- 'Set boundaries.'
- 'Stay calm and in control.'
- 'Be kind.'
- 'Watch how they like to be managed and how they best respond positively.'

11

Social media

The beep of your phone, vibration in your pocket and flash of a notification. Social media has been infiltrating our daily lives for over a decade and has divided opinion – do these platforms foster hate and abuse or will online communities create a better future?

At the beginning of 2018, there were 44 million social media users in the UK – 66% of the population. Globally, there are over one billion people active on Facebook, 330 million monthly active users on Twitter and 800 million on Instagram. The impact social media is having on our lives is growing at a rapid pace.

With the UK government raising concerns about how social media is being used, describing it as 'an easy place to transmit offensive or abusive content', it's important to look at how our online accounts – and mobile phones – impact on our lives and what we can do to keep it positive.

In 2017, a survey asked 1,479 young people aged 14–24 to score popular social media apps on issues such as anxiety, depression, loneliness, bullying, body image and 'fear of missing out'. YouTube was found to have the most positive impact on young people, while Instagram was deemed the most negative.

FOMO

Caterina Fake, an American entrepreneur and businesswoman popularized the term FOMO – fear of missing out – in 2011. 'It's an age-old problem, exacerbated by technology,' Caterina wrote on her blog. 'FOMO is a great motivator of human behaviour. Others have studied how the neurochemistry that keeps us checking Facebook every five minutes is similar to the neurochemistry fuelling addiction. Social media has made us even more aware of the things we are missing out on.'

We make decisions every day that benefit our happiness and we wouldn't question them half as much as we do if it weren't for social media. It can highlight the areas of our lives we feel we're 'failing' at.

Just a quick swipe shows me how many of my friends have checked in at cool restaurants, posting photos of their Saturday brunches with their partner or friends. I'm at home alone, still in my pyjamas, having just polished off leftover Chinese takeaway from last night...

But seriously, social media can be a dangerous place if you're feeling low and in a cycle of comparing yourself to others. What we see can leave us feeling bad about ourselves. And yet, we keep going back for more.

Why? There's the thrill of being the first to hear breaking news or share a meme. It's natural to want to be in the know. But it's not always beneficial to our mental well-being. If you're chasing news and trying to keep up with the entire population of Joneses, you're going to fail.

But there is another way…

In 2012, Caterina's friend, Anil Dash, blogger, explored the idea of FOMO further and came up with JOMO. The JOY of missing out. 'There can be, and should be, a blissful, serene enjoyment in knowing, and celebrating, that there are folks out there having the time of their life at something that you might have loved to be doing, but are simply skipping,' Anil wrote. 'Being the one in control of what moves me, what I feel obligated by, and what attachments I have to fleeting experiences is not an authority that I'm willing to concede to the arbitrary whims of an app on my mobile phone.'

I'm with Anil on this one. Give yourself permission to miss out. If people have big life news, you'll find out somehow. Some of my friends have NO social media accounts and yet we manage to stay in touch the old-fashioned way – texts and calls.

> 43% of people who took the kindfulness survey said they think they are addicted to social media – and 16% said they were a 'little bit' addicted.

Put your phone down

In 2017, a survey revealed more people made their New Year's resolution to spend less time on social media than made a resolution to get married, quit smoking or buy their first property.

I'm guilty of double or even triple screening on occasions – TV, laptop and phone all shining brightly. We overload our senses with technology and it's something we need to be more aware of.

For many years I've worked in the digital industry and know from experience how easy it can be to slip down the rabbit hole of social media accounts, websites, YouTube videos, and come up gasping for air hours later. Just one more clip, just one post, just one more…

Social media is addictive. When someone interacts with us – a like, a comment, a share – it stimulates a dopamine hit, the reward chemical released by the brain that motivates us to repeat that behaviour. So we keep going back for more.

It's a dangerous cycle to get caught up in. Being conscious of this and acknowledging how addictive online activity can be is key to breaking the cycle.

I love social media and was an early sign-up to Facebook, Twitter and Instagram (RIP my MySpace page!). And YouTube. And podcasts. I'm a consumer of stories and voices and pictures – from friends and strangers, people I admire and am intrigued by.

But I'm also aware of how much time I spend on these platforms. We've all got to cast some serious side-eye at social media and recognize the reverberations it can have on our well-being.

When was the last time you sat alone in a coffee shop, bar or restaurant waiting for a friend and didn't pull out your phone to kill 10 minutes? We're losing the art of doing nothing, of sitting with our thoughts and taking in our surroundings. Of having a few moments' peace.

Use moments of boredom when you'd usually start swiping to sit with your own thoughts. Embrace the art of doing nothing. Spend a few minutes taking in your surroundings. Listening to whatever is going on around you. Hell, let's bring back eavesdropping on strangers' conversations and NOT tweeting them!

Give your brain a moment to breathe. It's good for creativity, planning and daydreaming.

Don't let your phone get in the way of some mindful me time.

Got nothing to do? Instead of picking up your phone or opening your laptop, try one of these…

- Go for a walk in the park.

- Read that book your friend recommended.

- Run a bath and listen to some soothing music.

- Have a kitchen disco while cooking dinner.

- Arrange to meet a friend for a coffee – agree on a time and place and show up without your phones. Just like in the old days!

- Go on a day trip – only decide the destination on the way.

- Get all your favourite photos printed out and put together a photo album.

Print out extra copies for friends and family as presents.

◆ Watch your favourite film. In fact, watch three back to back. But make sure the TV is the only screen you're looking at.

> 60% of people who took the kindfulness survey said social media has had a positive impact on their life.

Love social media and still have a life

Put a time limit on it

Set your phone alarm if you have to. But, as I've established, social media can be addictive – be stricter with yourself.

Don't forget the people IRL

Your 'in real life' friends are worth infinitely more of your time and attention than a stranger's beauty blog or random goat video. If you have 10 minutes to kill, text someone you love. Or even better, write them a card and post it – really retro!

Don't push it

Refuse push notifications. The only ones I have are for text and WhatsApp messages and break-ing news alerts. I choose when I'll log in and check my accounts. Do not let your phone dictate when to get back to people with a beep.

Use your unfollow button

When I come across someone who is throwing around negativity like it's confetti at a wedding I simply unfollow. If they are offensive and abusive, I'll report and block. And then step away. Do not feed the trolls.

Follow your tribe

Make sure there's a good dose of reality in your social media feeds. If your body image isn't at its best (why not – you look gorgeous btw!), do NOT spend hours scrolling photos of Victoria's Secret models and comparing yourself to them. Find the people who are positive and make you feel good about yourself. The people who champion others rather than tear them down.

Find good news

Don't OD on news outlets. Good news rarely makes the headlines, so limit your time reading negative news stories that can cause stress, anxiety, fatigue or sleep loss. Keep abreast of what's going on in the world but follow accounts like @tanksgoodnews, which reminds us humanity does still exist.

Smoke and mirrors

The majority of social media users want to project their best lives out into the world. Which means followers get a false sense of who people are. Reality is skewed on social media, and it's important to remember that. From filters to photoshopping, celebrities have been slammed for faking it and being bad role models to their young fans. And then you have the people keeping it real: the positive body-image warriors and the 'he just pooed in the bath, I'm going to lose my shit' parent bloggers. I have such huge respect for everyone who keeps it authentic on social media.

Change your social media habits

Have regular breaks from your phone. If you're in a relationship and spend most evenings in silence checking your phones while watching TV, then vow to leave your phones in another room for a few hours each night.

Got 10 minutes to kill or half an hour to wait? Use that time to listen to a meditation app. Don't start scrolling.

Leave the house without your mobile. Take regular breaks from it, especially at the weekend. If the thought of being away from your phone fills you with fear, there's a problem. Introduce small periods of time when you leave it in another room and build up to leaving it at home completely.

Make sure push notifications are turned off. Turn your sound off too. It can be intrusive and disruptive.

Having a night out? Keep your phone in your bag or at least have it screen down on the table. I take photos on my phone on nights out but usually don't post anything until I'm on my way home or the next morning.

If a friend is constantly checking their phone, ask them politely to put it away. Suggest a no-phones rule so you can enjoy a proper catch-up.

Stop comparing yourself to others. It's a glimpse into their lives – often heavily filtered. So before you start thinking about how their life is so much greater than yours, remember it's just a snapshot.

Use your social media account for positive change. Champion charities, worthy causes and small businesses. Congratulate people on good news. Be yourself and have fun. And don't say anything you wouldn't say to a person face to face.

Don't beat yourself up if you still find yourself picking up your phone subconsciously. Just be more mindful of how much time you spend on social media. And maybe introduce other 'me time' habits into your life, which don't involve technology!

12

Be kind, be grateful

While your own happiness is key, there is a huge movement to bring more kindness into society at large. When the news is screaming scandal, global political crisis and gun violence, there's never been a more important time to show kindness towards others. And being kind has health benefits for you too.

A study at Sewanee: The University of the South, Tennessee, found that those who performed random acts of kindness were more likely to report feeling happy or having their mood boosted than participants who were just kind to themselves.

Studies and research also show the following:

+ Acts of kindness create an emotional warmth and protects the heart by lowering blood pressure.

+ People who regularly offer practical help to others have a lower risk of dying over a five-year period than those who do not.

+ Helping others relieves the signs and feelings of stress.

+ Spending money on others can make us feel better.

+ Those who provide support to friends have better self-esteem, less depression, and even lower blood pressure.

+ People who perform an act of kindness and gratitude towards another person immediately show a huge increase in happiness scores, and the benefits can last for a month after.

- ◆ Good deeds make people feel good about themselves and random acts of kindness are perfect as the novelty appears to be linked to happiness as well.

- ◆ Happiness increases simply by counting kindnesses performed over the course of a week. So when we think of the kind things we've done for others, we automatically feel happier ourselves.

- ◆ Meditating on a compassionate approach shifts activity in the brain to the area associated with happiness, and boosts immune functions.

Spreading kindfulness

We already have an annual worldwide Random Acts of Kindness Week, but what about the rest of the year?

Kindness is on the up. In 2018, research by Travelodge found 29% of those asked believe that performing a random act of kindness towards a stranger is good karma. It's certainly something

I believe in. When I see tourists struggling with directions I always offer to help them out, and often find locals more than happy to help when I'm travelling – 'map karma' is real!

The survey also found that a third of adults say a gesture of goodwill from a stranger makes them want to go out and help others. And it doesn't have to be a big favour, either: 75% of those asked believe it's the smallest act of kindness from a stranger that means the most.

Make it your mission to spread kindness. Pay it forward. Do a favour without expectation and I find it's paid back three-fold at some point.

Kindfulness gratitude journal

Keeping note of your gratitude is one of the best things you can do if you're looking to develop a more positive outlook. Studies have shown that showing gratitude in classrooms, at the dinner table or expressing it in a diary boosts happiness and social well-being and health.

The Bullet Journal movement, known as #bujo, has become popular recently. It's simply keeping a

'The simplest acts of kindness are far more powerful than a thousand heads bowing in prayer.'

Mahatma Gandhi

daily, monthly and annual journal of your goals and things you are grateful for. Keeping a gratitude journal every day and reflecting on your day will help you focus on the people and opportunities you have. The small moments that mean the most. It's a time to celebrate yourself and write down everything you managed to achieve. Listing things you are grateful for helps you find your happiness and, over time, should make you optimistic and positive.

Kindfulness survey

You say...

What are you most grateful for today?

Relationship
Cats Parents Partner Money to live Music
Happiness Boyfriend Kids
Good health
Food Love Education Pizza
Exercise Blue sky Job Snow
Wife Coffee
Cooking
Husband

My Kindfulness Diary

Every day, ask yourself two simple questions: How am I feeling today? What five things am I most grateful for?

Monday

Tuesday

Wednesday

Thursday

Friday

Saturday

Sunday

Kindfulness playlist

I've used Pink's *Raise Your Glass* to put me in a good mood on the way to work and Carole King's *Beautiful* to remind me of my self-worth. Here are just some of the songs on my kindfulness playlist…

This Is Me – The Greatest Showman
        (Original Motion Picture Soundtrack)
*F***ing Perfect* – Pink
Beautiful – Carole King
Break Out – Swing Out Sister
Change Your Life – Little Mix
Man in the Mirror – Michel Jackson
Don't Stop Me Now – Queen
Stronger – Kelly Clarkson
Roar – Katy Perry
I Will Survive – Gloria Gaynor
Respect – Aretha Franklin
Raise Your Glass – Pink
Born This Way – Lady Gaga
Express Yourself – Madonna
Shake It Off – Taylor Swift
Confident – Demi Lovato

Mean – Taylor Swift

Titanium – David Guetta and Sia

Cheerleader – OMI

Power – Little Mix

Fighter – Christina Aguilera

Hold My Hand – Jess Glynne

Run the World (Girls) – Beyoncé

Firework – Katy Perry

Survivor – Destiny's Child

Bulletproof – La Roux

Girl on Fire – Alicia Keys

Let It Go – Idina Menzel

No – Meghan Trainor

Before I go...

Dear YOU,

So we've come to the end, but that doesn't mean it's over between you and me. Hopefully we're just getting started.

Turn to pages 27–30. Look over your kindfulness PDR and see if you need to make any amendments to your plan of action.

Since applying kindfulness to my life, I'm the happiest I've ever been. My life is far from perfect, but I've realized 'perfection' is overrated anyway. Messy lives full of challenges and adventures, imperfections and mistakes with a huge serving of self-compassion, a dollop of confidence and a sprinkle of self-worth is the way forward. I'm done with guilt. I'm over shame. And I'm embracing all the random lessons life throws at me.

I hope kindfulness has given you the tools to make some positive changes in your life and spurred you into action to tackle that toxic friend, make your career work for you and give your relationship a happiness MOT. Be kind to yourself. You are enough.

Get in touch and let me know how you get on @showbizmillie!

Caroline
x

13

Sources
& organizations

Contributors

Mary Meadows – Performance life coach and NLP
practitioner @badasslifecoach

Nadia Essex – TV dating expert and love coach
@LadyNadiaEssex

Tom Read Wilson – dating guru from Celebs Go
Dating @TomReadWilson

Gemma Oaten – actress, singer and Patron of
SEED, Eating Disorder Support Services
seedeatingdisorders.org.uk @gemmaoaten

Anna Williamson – bestselling author of *Breaking Mad* and *Breaking Mum and Dad*, TV and radio presenter. www.annawilliamson.co.uk @awilliamsonTV

Camilla Sacre-Dallerup – life coach, hypnotherapist and bestselling author of *Reinvent Me*, www.zenme.tv @camillaDallerup

Catherine Gray – bestselling author of *The Unexpected Joy of Being Sober* @cathgraywrites

Annabelle Knight – Relationship expert and author, www.annabelleknight.com @MissBelleKnight

Organizations

www.mind.org.uk – Mind Infoline: 0300 123 3393

www.mentalhealth.org.uk

www.youngminds.org.uk – Helpline: 0808 802 5544

www.samaritans.org – Samaritans 116 123 (UK) 116 123 (ROI) jo@samaritans.org (UK) jo@samaritans.ie (ROI)

www.anxietyuk.org.uk –
  Helpline: 03444 775 774
  Mon-Fri 9:30am–5.30pm
  Text Service: 07537 416905

www.anxietyalliance.org.uk – Helpline: 0845 296
  7877 (10 a.m.–10 p.m. daily)

www.nopanic.org.uk – Helpline: 0844 967 4848

www.time-to-change.org.uk

www.rethink.org – 0300 5000 927

www.depressionuk.org

www.b-eat.co.uk – Helpline: 0808 801 0677;
  Youthline: 0808 801 0711

www.seedeatingdisorders.org.uk – Helpline: 01482
  718130

www.mengetedstoo.co.uk

www.oagb.org.uk

Thank yous

Firstly, thank you for reading *Kindfulness*. I hope it inspires you to treat yourself with more self-compassion and pass on the kindness.

Huge thanks to my brilliant agent Carly Cook for believing in me and *Kindfulness*. You're the best!

To my editor Ellen Parnavelas and all the team at Head of Zeus: Suzanne, Blake, Christina, Jennifer and Beth. THANK YOU. I look forward to doing it all over again!

The wonderful contributors who shared their wisdom and are truly kind people: Camilla Sacre-Dallerup, Anna Williamson, Gemma Oaten, Nadia Essex, Tom Read-Wilson, Annabelle Knight, Mary Meadows and Catherine Gray.

I'd also like to thank every person who took

the time to take part in the Kindfulness survey 2017 and share their own experiences.

My family. Mum and dad for their love, encouragement and support. Leanne, the kindest woman I know and the best big sister in the world. And my niblings Jake and Eliza for teaching me kindness through young eyes.

My friends. Ruth and Dave Vernon, James and Edward for being the kindest. And the fabulous Nick Boulos and Suzy Cox for being there when I needed them. To all my wonderful cheerleaders who got in formation and shook their pom poms for me – your love is always appreciated. The members of Monday Night Club and beyond. My fabulous CFTwo friends. Catherine Page for listening. I'm beyond grateful for all the support I have received while working on this book.

Finally, thank you to everyone who has ever shown me kindness. I hope you are as kind to yourselves.